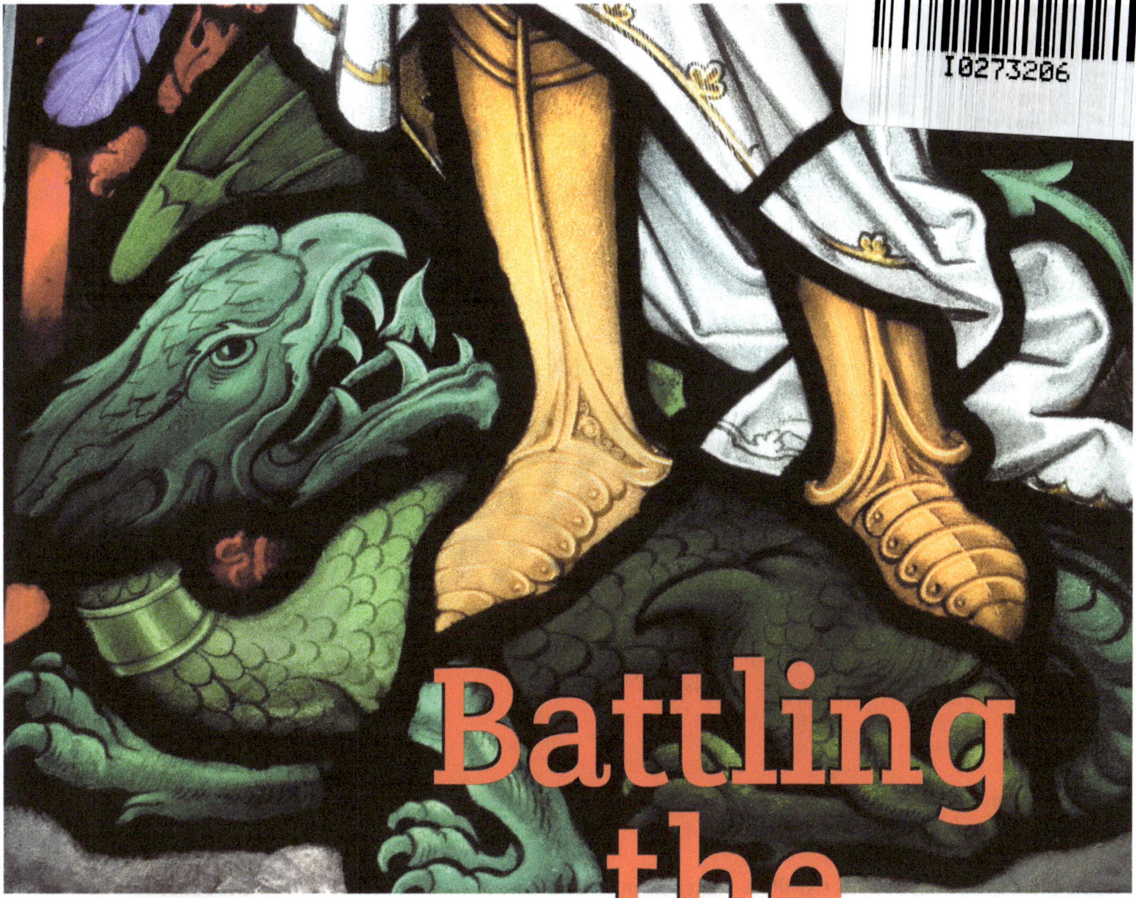

Battling the Dragon

A Prophetic Guide to Survival in the Last Days

Paul Haynes

ASPECT Books
www.ASPECTBooks.com

World rights reserved. This book or any portion thereof may not be copied or reproduced in any form or manner whatever, except as provided by law, without the written permission of the publisher, except by a reviewer who may quote brief passages in a review.

The author assumes full responsibility for the accuracy of all facts and quotations as cited in this book. The opinions expressed in this book are the author's personal views and interpretations, and do not necessarily reflect those of the publisher.

This book is provided with the understanding that the publisher is not engaged in giving spiritual, legal, medical, or other professional advice. If authoritative advice is needed, the reader should seek the counsel of a competent professional.

Copyright © Paul Haynes
Copyright © 2014 ASPECT Books
ISBN-13: 978-1-4796-0220-9 (Paperback)
ISBN-13: 978-1-4796-0221-6 (ePub)
ISBN-13: 978-1-4796-0222-3 (Mobi)
Library of Congress Control Number: 2014908218

All scripture quotations, unless otherwise indicated, are taken from the King James Version. Public domain.

Scripture quotations marked (AMP) are taken from the Amplified Bible, Copyright © 1954, 1958, 1962, 1964, 1965, 1987 by The Lockman Foundation. Used by permission.

Scripture quotations marked (NIV) are taken from the Holy Bible, New International Version®, NIV®. Copyright © 1973, 1978, 1984, 2011 by Biblica, Inc.™ Used by permission of Zondervan. All rights reserved worldwide.

Scripture quotations marked (NLT) are taken from the *Holy Bible,* New Living Translation, copyright © 1996, 2004, 2007 by Tyndale House Foundation. Used by permission of Tyndale House Publishers, Inc., Carol Stream, Illinois 60188. All rights reserved.

Scripture quotations marked (Weymouth) are from the *Weymouth New Testament*, Richard Francis Weymouth, 1912. Public domain in the United States.

Published by

Table of Contents

Chapter 1	A Call to Battle	5
Chapter 2	Enemy Intel	8
Chapter 3	The Dragon Attacks	12
Chapter 4	War Over Worship	19
Chapter 5	An Unholy Union	35
Chapter 6	God's Counter Attack	47
Chapter 7	Prophetic Jigsaw Puzzle	61
Chapter 8	Last-Day Timelines	78
Chapter 9	Same Enemies, Different Descriptions	93
Chapter 10	Victory Assured!	116
Chapter 11	Battling the Dragon with the Boldness of a Shepherd	118

Chapter 1

A Call to Battle

History is full of battles. Historians tell us where the battles took place, who the combatants and their leaders were, what strategy and weapons the armies used, and so forth. When God tells us about a battle, His greater interest is in our understanding the character of the combatants. The first battle mentioned in Scripture features the intervention of a peace-loving shepherd.

> Chedorlaomer, king of Elam, had invaded Canaan fourteen years before, and made it tributary to him. Several of the princes now revolted, and the Elamite king, [one of] four allies, again marched into the country to reduce them to submission. Five kings of Canaan joined their forces and met the invaders in the vale of Siddim, but only to be completely overthrown. A large part of the army was cut to pieces, and those who escaped fled for safety to the mountains. The victors plundered the cities of the plain and departed with rich spoil and many captives, among whom were Lot and his family. (Ellen G. White, *Patriarchs and Prophets*, p. 134)

Miraculously, one of Lot's men escaped and ran back to tell Abram the Hebrew, who was shepherding his large flocks in the plain near the oak groves belonging to Mamre the Amorite (Gen. 14:13). Abram had moved here to peacefully resolve conflict with his nephew over grazing territory. Lot did not seem to notice Abram's sacrifice. Yet, Abraham "cherished no unkind memory of Lot's ingratitude. All his affection for him was awakened, and he determined that he should be rescued. Seeking, first of all, divine counsel, [Abram] prepared for war" (*Patriarchs and Prophets*, p. 135). Abram's first action at hearing the news reveals his character. Falling to his knees, he asked counsel of his heavenly Father, and God's instruction was that he go after the captives. Confident that God was leading, Abraham prepared for war, mobilizing the trained men who had been born into his household and arming them for battle (Gen. 14:14).

> … From his own encampment he summoned three hundred and eighteen trained servants, men trained in the fear of God, in the service of their master, and in the practice

of arms. His confederates, Mamre, Eschol, and Aner, joined him with their bands, and together they started in pursuit of the invaders. (*Patriarchs and Prophets*, p. 135)

The men who lived in Abraham's camp had been trained to worship God and were obedient servants. They knew how to hoe and plant and provide for their families, and they also knew how to use the spear and the sword. Abraham's household army was supplemented by men under the command of Mamre, Eschol, and Aner. Together they pursued Chedorlaomer's army and his captives until they caught up with them at the valley of Shaveh in Dan (Gen. 14:17).

> ... The Elamites and their allies had encamped at Dan, on the northern border of Canaan. Flushed with victory, and having no fear of an assault from their vanquished foes, they had given themselves up to reveling. (*Patriarchs and Prophets*, p. 135)

The victorious army of the five kings had let down their guard and Abraham took advantage of this.

> ... The patriarch divided his force so as to approach from different directions, and came upon the encampment by night. His attack, so vigorous and unexpected, resulted in speedy victory. The king of Elam was slain and his panic-stricken forces were utterly routed. Lot and his family, with all the prisoners and their goods, were recovered, and a rich booty fell into the hands of the victors. (*Patriarchs and Prophets*, p. 135)

Were it not for this peace-loving shepherd of God, the rescue would not have taken place.

> ... To Abraham, under God, the triumph was due. The worshiper of Jehovah had not only rendered a great service to the country, but had proved himself a man of valor. It was seen that righteousness is not cowardice, and that Abraham's religion made him courageous in maintaining the right and defending the oppressed. His heroic act gave him a widespread influence among the surrounding tribes. (*Patriarchs and Prophets*, p. 135)

Not only did Abraham provide for and protect his family and camp, but he also accepted the responsibility of maintaining the right and defending the oppressed.

Those who use force and arms to obtain their own desires and oppress the weak and defenseless for their own gain are the enemies of God. They can expect God's retribution under His servants. In the story in Genesis 14, a quiet and peace-loving shepherd answered God's call and re-established the right, saving the captives.

This same call belongs to the people of God at the present time. God has given us a picture of His enemy in the prophecies of Daniel and Revelation, and He is asking us to drop our peaceful activities and prepare for war. He is asking us to re-establish the law of God and save those who have been taken captive by His enemy.

Yet, before we take up the battle, we must do as Abram did and seek the Lord.

> "Father, I am not a soldier, and I do not know how to engage the enemy. However, I know this: I belong to You. Train me, Lord. Help me to get ready. Then send me to help fight this battle with You and for You."

Chapter 2
Enemy Intel

To gain intelligence on the enemy, we begin a reconnaissance mission into the Garden of Eden just after God created it and placed Adam and Eve within it. It was in paradise that the enemy of God first made himself known through one of many guises.

> Now the serpent was more subtle than any beast of the field which the Lord God had made. And he said unto the woman, Yea, hath God said, Ye shall not eat of every tree of the garden? (Gen. 3:1)

Surprised to hear another creature speaking to her, the woman answered:

> We may eat of the fruit of the trees of the garden: But of the fruit of the tree which is in the midst of the garden, God hath said, Ye shall not eat of it, neither shall ye touch it, lest ye die. (Gen. 3:2, 3)

Undaunted, the serpent responded: "Ye shall not surely die: For God doth know that in the day ye eat thereof, then your eyes shall be opened, and ye shall be as gods, knowing good and evil" (Gen. 3:4, 5)

> And when the woman saw that the tree was good for food, and that it was pleasant to the eyes, and a tree to be desired to make one wise, she took of the fruit thereof, and did eat, and gave also unto her husband with her; and he did eat. And the eyes of them both were opened, and they knew that they were naked; and they sewed fig leaves together, and made themselves aprons. (Gen. 3:6, 7)

This narrative from Genesis tells us how Eve wandered near the tree of good and evil and found herself talking with a beautiful serpent. She was curious about the tree—but even more curious to hear such a beautiful and intelligent creature addressing her as she approached. The serpent asks her why she is not eating of the tree of good and evil. Eve tells him that God has told them not to eat of it. The serpent counters that she will not die from eating of the tree. In fact, he says, the fruit has special powers. In eating it, she will become like God. Eve considers the words of this beautiful creature made by God, and the inordinate desire to be like God arises in her heart, and she decides that she must have some of the fruit. Hastily she takes a piece of fruit and eats it. The fruit tastes wonderful and she imagines herself taking on new powers. Gathering more fruit, she finds her husband, and offers some to him. He also considers his choices and partakes of the fruit.

The Bible then tells us the result of their acts of rebellion against God: their eyes are opened; they realized that they are naked; they now know good and evil (Gen. 3:7). Nervously they clothe themselves with fig leaves. Yet, the God who sees all knows what they have done and comes looking for them. The biblical narrative continues.

> And the LORD God called unto Adam, and said unto him, Where art thou? And he said, I heard thy voice in the garden, and I was afraid, because I was naked; and I hid myself. And he said, Who told thee that thou wast naked? Hast thou eaten of the tree, whereof I commanded thee that thou shouldest not eat? And the man said, The woman whom thou gavest to be with me, she gave me of the tree, and I did eat. And the LORD God said unto the woman, What is this that thou hast done? And the woman said, The serpent beguiled me, and I did eat. And the LORD God said unto the serpent, Because thou hast done this, thou art cursed above all cattle, and above every beast of the field; upon thy belly shalt thou go, and dust shalt thou eat all the days of thy life: And I will put enmity between thee and the woman, and between thy seed and her seed; it shall bruise thy head, and thou shalt bruise his heel. (Gen. 3:9–15)

The tree was a test of their loyalty to God. Both Adam and Eve knew what God expected. His command was simple:. Do not eat the fruit of that one particular tree. Yet, in spite of God's explicit commandment, they decided to listen to the serpent and eat the fruit. Adam and Eve's crime was also simple: they did what they were asked not to do. They sinned against God's command, and they received the consequences of their action. God pronounced curses upon them and upon the earth because of their actions (Gen. 3:14–19).

Among these curses is the judgment that fell upon the serpent. Because the serpent led our parents into sin, God told him that he would crawl on his belly and eat the dust of the earth all the days of his life. The freedom of flight was no longer his. Then God gives a prophecy that concerns the serpent and Adam and Eve's offspring. God tells the serpent that the Savior of man will arise within Eve's descendants. This Savior of man will crush the head of the serpent after the serpent has bruised the Savior's heel.

Is God a "serpent whisperer," sentencing the serpent to punishment for his evil deeds? Was there not someone else He was addressing in speaking to the serpent? The last book of the Bible indicates that the serpent represented more than a slithering reptile. Revelation 12:3 refers to "a great red dragon." Revelation 12:9 identifies him as "*that old serpent*, called the Devil, and Satan, which deceiveth the whole world." The passage says that the dragon pursues a woman, who is clothed with the sun.

That dragon identified as "that old serpent" points back to the serpent that tempted Eve in the Garden of Eden. In other words, in Genesis 3, God was addressing Satan, who was behind the serpent. Somehow Satan had gained control of the serpent's mouth to set up his encounter with Eve. The body was that of a serpent, but the serpent's actions and words were those of Satan.

Returning to the garden, we see that it was Satan who tempted Eve, who then carried the temptation to her husband. In eating the fruit that they had been told not to eat, Adam and Eve disobeyed the word of their Creator. They had chosen to believe the words of the serpent, who we now know was none other than Satan himself. Their actions declare whom they listened to—the serpent instead of their Creator. These actions are sin, and the consequences of their sinning was the loss of their home in Eden and of their lives. Yet, God did not leave them in a hopeless condition. In the promise of the crushing of the serpent's head, He gave them the promise of the gospel, which guarantees eternal life to those who believe in the Son of God. Yet, before the serpent's head is crushed, there will be a horrific war.

Revelation 12 described the expulsion of Satan from heaven. He was cast out of heaven for the same crime as that of Adam and Eve. He had turned from the worship of God to the worship of himself. After the first encounter with man, he was cast to the earth for his actions against the children of God. Because Adam and Eve bowed in worship to the serpent, Satan claimed the earth as his property. Yet, the seed of the woman would come to earth to win it back.

After the story of the fall of man by Satan's deceiving Adam and Eve through lies, Satan's next major appearance on earth is in the story of the second Adam's temptations in the wilderness.

> Then was Jesus led up of the Spirit into the wilderness to be tempted of the devil. And when he had fasted forty days and forty nights, he was afterward an hungered. And when the tempter came to him, he said, If thou be the Son of God, command that these stones be made bread. But he answered and said, It is written, Man shall not live by bread alone, but by every word that proceedeth out of the mouth of God. Then the devil taketh him up into the holy city, and setteth him on a pinnacle of the temple, And saith unto him, If thou be the Son of God, cast thyself down: for it is written, He shall give his angels charge concerning thee: and in their hands they shall bear thee up, lest at any time thou dash thy foot against a stone. Jesus said unto him, It is written again, Thou shalt not tempt the Lord thy God. Again, the devil taketh him up into an exceeding high mountain, and showeth him all the kingdoms of the world, and the glory of them; And saith unto him, All these things will I give thee, if thou wilt fall down and worship me. Then saith Jesus unto him, Get thee hence, Satan: for it is written, Thou shalt worship the Lord thy God, and him only shalt thou serve. Then the devil leaveth him, and, behold, angels came and ministered unto him. (Matt. 4:1–11)

We read here that the tempter, now posing as an angel of light, comes to Jesus after He has been fasting for about forty days. Twice Jesus meets the angel's temptations with the words of Scripture, refusing to budge from strict obedience to His Father's direction. Revealing his true nature, Satan tries… one time more. The third temptation is the most profound, yet blatant. The tempter promises that if Jesus will worship him, he will hand over the sovereignty of the world to Him.

The questions is simple, Will you worship me instead of God? Jesus sees and understands. He responds by calling the tempter by his name—Satan, a name that means "adversary." Though Satan was masquerading as an angel of God, Jesus reveals that He is able to see through Satan's disguise. The words of this angel of light have betrayed him. He is none other than Satan, the enemy of God. Besides calling him by name, Jesus repeats a principle of life from heaven: God is the only one created beings should worship, and He is the one we should listen to and obey.

Adam and Eve had been servants of God, but sin made them servants of Satan. In the narrative of the temptations in Matthew, we read that Jesus passed the test of loyalty that Adam and Eve failed. The "last Adam" (1 Cor. 15:45) passed the test of loyalty to God. He knew who Satan was and won back that which had been lost in Eden. Satan tried to destroy Adam and Eve, and he tried to destroy Jesus. We too must realize that this enemy of God is trying to destroy us. We must recognize that Satan is our adversary and the enemy of God. It is our job to remove his mask.

Satan presented himself to Eve in the guise of a beautiful serpent. She was overcome by deceit. He presented himself to Jesus as an angel of light, descended from the throne of God (cf. 2 Cor. 11:14). But Jesus trusted in the word of God, and He was victorious over the lies of the devil.

Revelation tells us that Satan will appear on earth a third time. How will he appear? Will he put on the guise of a serpent, or will he look like an angel of God? What will he say to try to lead humans from the path that God has given us?

Revelation tells us that Satan will use kingdoms and armies, the false teachings of religious institutions, and supernatural power to turn the heads of the people of the world from God to himself. Though the issue will be the same as in the Garden of Eden with Adam and Eve and in the wilderness with Jesus, this time Satan will confront the whole world. Whom will human beings worship—Satan or God? Preparing for that confrontation is the purpose of this book.

> "Father in heaven, thank you for the example of our Savior. Help us to get ready for this final confrontation with the enemy of life through the careful study of Revelation. Stay by our side and guide our words, thoughts, and actions. Amen."

Chapter 3
The Dragon Attacks

Before the death of John, who was the last of the apostles, Jesus gave His servant prophetic visions of what was to come. As we consider John's visions in the book of Revelation, given nearly two thousand years ago, you will come to the startling realization that the book was written for people living on earth today. It is my belief that the prophecies of Revelation we will consider in this book are to be fulfilled in the future. In the next few chapters, you will find that God has given specific identifying characteristics of the enemies of Christ.

Let's begin. In vision, John saw a dramatic representation:

> And there appeared a great wonder in heaven; a woman clothed with the sun, and the moon under her feet, and upon her head a crown of twelve stars: And she being with child cried, travailing in birth, and pained to be delivered. (Rev. 12:1, 2)

John noticed that the woman seen in the vision was pregnant and ready to give birth. What does this symbolize? The notes of Methodist commentator Adam Clarke help us understand the language that John used to describe the scene:

> That the woman here represents the true Church of Christ most commentators are agreed. In other parts of the Apocalypse, the pure Church of Christ is evidently portrayed by a woman. In chap. xix., ver. 7, a great multitude are represented as saying, "Let us be glad and rejoice, and give honour to him; for the marriage of the Lamb is come, and his wife hath made herself ready." In chap. xxi. 9, an angel talks with St. John, saying, "Come hither, I will show thee the bride, the Lamb's wife." That the Christian Church is meant will appear also from her being *clothed with the sun*, a striking emblem of Jesus Christ, the Sun of righteousness, the light and glory of the Church; for the countenance of the Son of God is *as the sun shineth in his strength*.... (Adam Clarke, *The New Testament of Our Lord and Saviour Jesus Christ, with a Commentary and Critical Notes* [New York: T. Mason & G. Lane, 1837], vol. 2, pp. 1008, 1009)

The Dragon Attacks

Along with many other commentators, Adam Clarke believed that the woman introduced in this chapter symbolizes the church of Christ. Let us use that idea to try to make sense of the description in Revelation. First, her character is obvious. She is "clothed with the sun" and standing on the moon. Genesis 1:16 says: "God made two great lights; the greater light to rule the day, and the lesser light to rule the night…." Adam Clarke proposed that this analogy describes Jesus, for Revelation 1:16 says the countenance of the Son of God is "as the sun shineth in his strength." Would this symbolism not also apply to the description of the church of Christ? The moon under the church's feet reflects the light of the Sun. This means that God's people reflect Christ's character.

John also tells us that the woman was wearing a crown of twelve stars. The crown signifies that she is a queen. She holds an honored position beside the King of kings. As we have noted, the woman is not only pregnant, but she is in labor. This painful experience culminates in the birth of a new life. After this is another dramatic representation:

> And there appeared another wonder in heaven; and behold a great red dragon, having seven heads and ten horns, and seven crowns upon his heads. And his tail drew the third part of the stars of heaven, and did cast them to the earth: and the dragon stood before the woman which was ready to be delivered, for to devour her child as soon as it was born. (Rev. 12:3, 4)

Any thoughts of a peaceful existence, enjoying life in a country home with family and children, are dashed by this violent scene. The enemy is depicted as a great red dragon with seven heads, ten horns, and seven crowns on the heads. John watched as the dragon took one third of the stars of heaven and cast them to the earth. Earlier in Revelation, Jesus told John that stars are symbols of angels (Rev. 1:20). As applied here, the stars are angels created by God who allied themselves with the red dragon and were cast out of heaven to the earth. What happens next in the vision is amazing: the dragon stands before the woman ready to pounce on her child and devour it as soon as it is born. Who will help the woman? Who will protect her innocent and defenseless newborn? John's account continues:

> And she brought forth a man child, who was to rule all nations with a rod of iron: and her child was caught up unto God, and to his throne. And the woman fled into the wilderness, where she hath a place prepared of God, that they should feed her there a thousand two hundred and threescore days. (Rev. 12:5, 6)

God reveals to John that, after the child is born, the dragon is not able to harm either mother or child. In reading the rest of the chapter, we will realize that it is the power of God that protects them. So who is the child? John identifies Him for us. He is the one who will rule all nations "with a rod of iron." Ruling with a rod of iron means bringing judgment, as we see in Revelation 2:27; 19:15; and Psalm 2:9. The man-child was caught up unto the throne of God in heaven. After this, John sees the woman flee into the wilderness, where she is given a place prepared by God. God feeds and protects her there for 1,260 days.

The narrative describes the child and the church. The woman dressed in the glory of the sun is a fitting symbol of the church of God, for, after Jesus' ascension, she was persecuted as predicted.

In the description of the child's birth and ascension to God, we see the story of man's Redeemer and Savior (Acts 1:11; Eph. 4:8–10). Scripture tells us that He is now in heaven serving as our High Priest (Heb. 4:15; 7:25). Yet, John's vision does not stop with Jesus' being called back to heaven. John continues with the description of the dragon's attack on the church of God. He tells us that he saw the woman, the church of Christ, flee into the wilderness to escape the wrath of the dragon. As we read through the rest of the chapter and into the following ones, we will recognize that God provided John details about the actions of the enemy of Christ. The focus of chapter 12 is not on the church's mission, but it is on the aggressive, hateful actions of the red dragon.

How did God keep the dragon from harming Jesus when the dragon waited at the birth of Jesus to kill Him? Matthew mentions God's protecting the babe through a dream (Matt. 2:13) and the presence of God's angels for Jesus' protection during His earthly ministry (cf. Matt. 26:53). Revelation says that, after Jesus ascends to heaven, the dragon will set his sights on the woman that he might destroy her. However, God protects the woman by sending her into the wilderness for 1,260 days.

God has a church on earth that He protects and watches over as His bride. He promised Adam and Eve that a Savior would arise to save human beings from their sins. That Savior is Jesus, the Son of God, who lived life on earth as the Son of man. He also died on the cross, rose from the dead, and is now in heaven (1 Cor. 15:3, 4; 1 Peter 3:21, 22). Yet, the joy of knowing what Jesus came to accomplish is overshadowed by the message of this vision. The church is in a deadly conflict with the enemy of God. The vision tells us that the woman was hunted by the dragon for 1,260 days. It also tells us that what the dragon tried to do to the newborn babe, he is trying to do to Christ's church. He is trying to destroy all who belong to Jesus.

The rest of chapter tells what comes after the 1,260 days. Though we have the promise of life in Jesus because He lived and died for us, yet the enemy will continue to wage war with the family of God until sin is removed from the universe forever.

How did the war begin? Verses 7 through 9 of Revelation 12 provide the backstory, which helps us understand what made it necessary for the Son of God to become the Savior of humankind.

> And there was war in heaven: Michael and his angels fought against the dragon; and the dragon fought and his angels, and prevailed not; neither was their place found any more in heaven. And the great dragon was cast out, that old serpent, called the Devil, and Satan, which deceiveth the whole world: he was cast out into the earth, and his angels were cast out with him. (Rev. 12:7–9)

Here, the theme of the chapter suddenly changes. God is giving John background information on the red dragon. Long before the dragon pursued the woman and her child, there had been war in heaven because of the dragon. The lines of battle were drawn between Michael and his angels and the dragon and his angels.

But who is Michael? Jude 1:9 calls Michael "the archangel." 1 Thessalonians 4:16 says that Jesus will "descend from heaven with a shout, *with the voice of the archangel*, and with the trump of God: and the dead in Christ shall rise first." John 5:25 says that the voice that raises the dead is "*the voice of the Son of God.*" Thus, Michael, the commander of the angels, is none other than Jesus Christ, the Son of God. As we have seen, the dragon is Satan, the original serpent in Eden.

Why was there war? Why would one who was an angel of God fight against Jesus, the Son of God? Satan went to war against the Son of God because he had chosen to walk in his own path rather than the path of God. Isaiah describes how Lucifer, an angel of light, fell from heaven:

> How art thou fallen from heaven, O Lucifer, son of the morning! how art thou cut down to the ground, which didst weaken the nations! For thou hast said in thine heart, I will ascend into heaven, I will exalt my throne above the stars of God: I will sit also upon the mount of the congregation, in the sides of the north: I will ascend above the heights of the clouds; I will be like the most High. (Isa. 14:12–14)

Lucifer's heart turned from worship of God to prideful worship of himself. Worship of self became the controlling power in his life and turned him from God. Lucifer's rebellion led God to take the next step. Since Lucifer, the light bearer, had become Satan, "the adversary," God cast him and the angels who were loyal to him out of heaven. John identifies the specific place to which Satan and his angels were cast—"he was cast out into the earth, and his angels were cast out with him" (Rev. 12:9).

So what is Satan doing on planet Earth? "Woe to the inhabiters of the earth and of the sea! for the devil is come down unto you, having great wrath, because he knoweth that he hath but a short time" (Rev. 12:12). Satan is depicted as a wild beast, looking for prey. "Be sober, be vigilant; because your adversary the devil, as a roaring lion, walketh about, seeking whom he may devour" (1 Peter 5:8). God's representation of Satan as a great red dragon ready to pounce on a newborn baby is a vivid reminder of the character of the enemy of God. Though Satan wants to destroy the children of God, God does not leave them unprotected. Returning to John's vision, we read:

> And I heard a loud voice saying in heaven, Now is come salvation, and strength, and the kingdom of our God, and the power of his Christ: for the accuser of our brethren is cast down, which accused them before our God day and night. And they overcame him by the blood of the Lamb, and by the word of their testimony; and they loved not their lives unto the death. Therefore rejoice, ye heavens, and ye that dwell in them. (Rev. 12:10–12)

Satan and his angels were exiled to planet Earth, their prison-house. It was Satan who deceived Eve and caused her to sin. He is the one who causes all to sin. Yet, that is not all. He looks back at God and mocks Him. He says, *Look at what You have created. Human beings were made in Your image. Yet, they are now sinning. How will You judge them? Will You destroy them?*

God's answer is simple. A voice calls out: "Now is come salvation, and strength, and the kingdom of our God, and the power of his Christ" (Rev. 12:10). When Jesus came to this earth, it was to purchase salvation for the human family. Jesus came to bring humankind strength to overcome evil. Salvation for humanity began with God's promise to Adam and Eve. At the cross, Jesus earned the right to be our Savior. John declares that, at the cross, Satan was cast down to the earth a second time.

Paul declares that Jesus openly triumphed over the devil and his angels on the cross (Col. 2:15). At the cross of Christ, God gave all human beings the opportunity to overcome sin and Satan "by the blood of the Lamb, and by the word of their testimony ..." (Rev. 12:11). What are the inhabitants of heaven to do with this knowledge? "Therefore rejoice, ye heavens, and ye that dwell in them" (Rev. 12:12). The Savior has overcome sin for humankind! Yet, the vision does not stop there, for the dragon did not surrender at the cross. The spiritual war continues.

Revelation 12:13 describes Satan's activity since he was cast out at the cross. "And when the dragon saw that he was cast unto the earth, he persecuted the woman which brought forth the man child." Did the woman perish under this persecution? The next verse answers: "And to the woman were given two wings of a great eagle, that she might fly into the wilderness, into her place, where she is nourished for a time, and times, and half a time, from the face of the serpent" (Rev. 12:14).

Once again the church was sent into the wilderness. This time John describes the time period as "a time, and times, and half a time." The word "time" is used for the passing of one sanctuary year, which equals 360 days (Dan. 4:16, 25). Adding up the components of the phrase, "a time, and times, and half a time" (a year + two years + half a year), we arrive at 1,260 days—the same period in verse 6. Since sanctuary "time" goes from one Day of Atonement to the next, this 1,260-day period is actually 1,260 prophetic sanctuary years. John is saying in this verse that the church will be nourished for 1,260 years. God provides food, shelter, and protection in the wilderness of the earth for His people for a period of 1,260 years. After this time, the red dragon will come against the church of God again:

> And the serpent cast out of his mouth water as a flood after the woman, that he might cause her to be carried away of the flood. And the earth helped the woman, and the earth opened her mouth, and swallowed up the flood which the dragon cast out of his mouth. (Rev. 12:15, 16)

The dragon produces a flood to destroy the woman, but God opens the earth to swallow up the flood. What does the symbolic language in this chapter mean? It tells us that Satan will do everything he can to destroy the church of Christ. He stops at nothing. Rather than yielding in the battle against God, Satan releases an overwhelming torrent of words and terror on the church to carry the church away to destruction. What is amazing is that God does not need to use armies and nuclear bombs to stop the attack. John watches as God uses the earth as His weapon of defense, opening its mouth to swallow "up the flood which the dragon cast out of his mouth." Yet, the battle against sin and Satan rages on.

Besides the earth's defense of the woman, Isaiah describes another solution for the dragon's gigantic flood:

> So shall they fear the name of the Lord from the west, and his glory from the rising of the sun. *When the enemy shall come in like a flood, the Spirit of the Lord shall lift up a standard against him.* (Isa. 59:19, emphasis supplied)

When the enemy of souls tries to overpower the church of Christ with a flood of false teachers and doctrines, God lifts up His "standard." In ancient Israel, each tribe had a standard placed before it. The standard represented the major character strength of the tribe. The standard mentioned in Isaiah is the most powerful weapon in God's arsenal. It is His character in the hearts of His children. The Lord God is mighty. During the time of the end, He will reveal His character to the world through His children. He will raise up His church as a standard against the flood of lies and false doctrines of the enemy.

When God's Son walked on the earth, the dragon tried to destroy Him. Jesus tells us, in Revelation 12, what happens when the dragon becomes furious with the woman at the time of the end: "And the dragon was wroth with the woman, and went to make war with the remnant of her seed, which keep the commandments of God, and have the testimony of Jesus Christ" (Rev. 12:17). During the Dark Ages, the dragon tried to destroy God's church. Now, at the time of the end, he will try to destroy God's standard—His people—openly. No longer will he work in the shadows, but he will show himself to the world in the light of day. This will be Satan's third appearance. Through words and miracles, he will win the allegiance of the world. With the world's adoration, he will publicly declare war on those who oppose him.

John uses the term "the remnant of her seed" to describe the remainder of God's faithful people. He clarifies who this includes by adding that they are the ones who "keep the commandments of God, and have the testimony of Jesus Christ." Now we understand what Isaiah was referring to when he said that God would raise up a standard against the flood of the dragon. These faithful followers of God are the standard that He will raise up at the time of the end. The character of the woman and her children is the issue for the enemy of God. Yet, what is so important for us to understand in this vision of Revelation 12?

The church of Christ is attacked by the beast, but God will protect His faithful ones. God protected His church during the ministry of Jesus. He protected His church during the middle ages. He will protect His church at the time of the end.

This beast does not cease his attacks upon the faithful. Through pagan Rome, this beast worked to destroy the Christ child. Through papal Rome, this beast worked during the Middle Ages to destroy the church of God. Through spiritualism this beast will work at the end of time to destroy the church of God. This beast will stand in the holy place in Jerusalem at the end of time, thinking that he has destroyed the church of God.

Revelation 12 says the red dragon was "cast out" out of heaven. In the Gospel of Luke, Jesus said that He "beheld Satan as lighting fall from heaven" (Luke 10:18). Revelation 12 identifies the great red dragon as "that old serpent, called the Devil and Satan." Matthew, Mark, Luke, and John describe the dragon's attempts to kill the Son of God (Luke 4:29; John 8:59; 10:31; Matt. 27:35; Mark 15:25; Luke 23:33; John 19:18). Yet, Jesus completed His work on earth and was called back to heaven. In Revelation, John says the dragon attacked the church of God for 1,260 years. He did this through pagan and papal Rome. Yet, God protected His church in the wilderness. John also says the dragon will flood the church with persecution and false doctrine. Yet, God will intervene and allow the earth to swallow the flood and keep Christ's bride safe.

Finally, John tells us that the red dragon gets so mad that he will declare war with the remnant of the church of God. We have read that he has been trying to destroy them for thousands of years, but at this point in time, he takes the final step. We will find out in the next chapter that he will have the whole world on his side. We will find out that he and the world will war against the people of God in one great final conflict.

Will this last battle on earth be like a football or baseball game with equal numbers on both sides? We know the answer. John tells us that Satan and the world will make war against "the remnant" of the church of God. Remnant means the last small portion. Why them? John tells us. He says that they will be known by two characteristics. They will have the word of God and the prophecies of Jesus Christ. Like John, they will have a work to do for God. They are His representatives on earth. We also know them as the riders of Revelation 6.

This vision of the enemies of Christ continues with Revelation 13. We will learn that the dragon and two of the three kingdoms introduced in Revelation 13 will make up the religious union known as Babylon. God will reveal some of the secrets of Satan's final plan. We will learn that this information is a warning for us. The angels of God are telling us to get ready, get ready, get ready!

> "Father, please give us enough time to get ready. Give us enough time to warn our families and friends and neighbors. Help us to get ready."

Chapter 4

War Over Worship

John has just finished describing his vision of the red dragon of Revelation 12. That beast had seven heads, ten horns, and seven crowns on the seven heads. We learned about the character of the red dragon when we were told that it tried to devour the newborn baby of the woman of Revelation 12. It then persecuted this woman for 1,260 years. After it tries to destroy the woman with a flood, John tells us that the final act of this beast will be to declare war on the children of God at the time of the end. So ends Revelation 12.

Revelation 13 is part of the same vision. We will find that these descriptions of beasts in chapters 12 and 13 are actually one vision. It depicts "beasts" that will impact history at the time of the end. Before exploring what the Bible says about these, we first need to define the word "beast" within the context of the chapter.

> beast—*Greek*, "wild beast." Man becomes "brutish" when he severs himself from God, the archetype and true ideal, in whose image he was first made, which ideal is realized by the man Christ Jesus. Hence, the world-powers seeking their own glory, and not God's, are represented as *beasts* …. (Robert Jamieson, Andrew Robert Fausset, and David Brown, *A Commentary, Critical and Explanatory, on the Old and New Testaments* [Toledo, OH: Jerome B. Names & Co., 1884], vol. 2, p. 592)

Jamieson, Fausset, and Brown note that the Greek word translated "beast" means "wild beast" and that it symbolizes "world powers seeking their own glory, and not God's." The four "beasts" described in Revelation 12 and 13 are "world powers" that are Satan's slaves. I will use the term to refer to each opponent of God and His people in chapters 12, 13, and 17. They will be the dominant forces at the time of the end. We have already covered chapter 12. Now we will continue with chapter 13.

The Composite Beast, Which Comes Out of the Sea

Beginning with verse 1, we read: "And I stood upon the sand of the sea, and saw a beast rise up out of the sea, having seven heads and ten horns, and upon his horns ten crowns, and upon his heads the name of blasphemy" (Rev. 13:1). This beast is like the red dragon in that it has seven heads and ten horns. However, unlike the dragon, it has *ten* crowns for its ten horns and the name of blasphemy on its seven heads. Besides these differences, John has to combine features of several animals to describe the beast. "And the beast which I saw was like unto a leopard, and his feet were as the feet of a bear, and his mouth as the mouth of a lion: and the dragon gave him his power, and his seat, and great authority" (Rev. 13:2). Why does this beast have features of a leopard, a bear, and a lion? It is because these are symbols from Daniel's vision in Daniel 7:

> The first was like a *lion*, and had eagle's wings: I beheld till the wings thereof were plucked, and it was lifted up from the earth, and made stand upon the feet as a man, and a man's heart was given to it. And behold another beast, a second, like to a *bear*, and it raised up itself on one side, and it had three ribs in the mouth of it between the teeth of it: and they said thus unto it, Arise, devour much flesh. After this I beheld, and lo another, like a *leopard*, which had upon the back of it four wings of a fowl; the beast had also four heads; and dominion was given to it. After this I saw in the night visions, and behold a fourth beast, *dreadful and terrible*, and strong exceedingly; and it had great iron teeth: it devoured and brake in pieces, and stamped the residue with the feet of it: and it was diverse from all the beasts that were before it; and it had *ten horns*. (Dan. 7:4–7, emphasis supplied)

Daniel 7 describes Daniel's vision about four beasts. The first was like a lion; the second was like a bear; the third was like a leopard. The fourth beast was dreadful and terrible. An angel from heaven gave Daniel the interpretation of these symbols: "These great beasts, which are four, are four kings, which shall arise out of the earth" (Dan. 7:17).

These wild beasts represent four kingdoms—four world powers—that were to rule the earth. The four kingdoms are Babylon, Medo-Persia, Greece, and pagan Rome. The beast that arises from the sea in Revelation 13 is a composite of the beasts in Daniel 7. Even though it is a unique power in history, it has inherited and assimilated the physical and spiritual characteristics of Babylon, Medo-Persia, Greece, and Rome—the powers that preceded it. It has the body of a leopard, the feet of a bear, and the mouth of a lion. In other words, it has the power and speed of a mighty leopard (representing Greece, cf. Dan. 8:21), it has the strong foundation of a bear (representing Medo-Persia, cf. Dan. 8:20), and, when it speaks, it grabs attention like a roaring lion (representing Babylon).

In order to identify this composite beast, we need to consider what John says next in his narrative. In verse 2, John tells us "the dragon gave" the first beast of Revelation 13 "his power, and his seat, and great authority." The dragon symbolized the power that ruled the world at the time of Christ. That historical power is pagan Rome. It is this power that gives the composite beast "his power, and his seat, and great authority" (Rev. 13:1). It is notable that the composite beast did not have to fight for its place in the sun like Babylon, Medo-Persia, Greece, and Rome; it was *given* its power. Hundreds of years after the passing of John, this is just what happened. It dominated world politics from AD 538 until 1798, when it received a mortal wound. These historical characteristics indicate that the composite beast is papal Rome. In the following verses in Revelation 13, John describes the attack and mortal wound of the composite beast:

> And I saw one of his heads as it were wounded to death; and his deadly wound was healed: and all the world wondered after the beast. And they worshipped the dragon which gave power unto the beast: and they worshipped the beast, saying, Who is like unto the beast? who is able to make war with him? (Rev. 13:3, 4)

This description implies that the wounded head of the beast should have caused the beast's sudden and immediate death. In 1798, the French General Berthier went to the Vatican and took Pope Pius VI captive. Pius VI died in captivity in 1799, yet the papacy did not come to an end. In the prophecy of Revelation 13, the wounded head of the beast revives. Because the great red dragon gave the beast its power and is praised when the beast's wound is healed, it must be responsible for saving it from death. Would you not call this healing a miracle?

John prophesied that this mortally wounded world power would rise again. He says that when this healing occurs, it was to be so astounding that "all the world" would wonder after the beast (Rev. 13:3). Those who wonder after it are not just the people in Rome or Italy, in Europe or Latin America, all the world is to wonder after the beast! Their reaction is not a simple matter of admiration or cheers. John says that the people of the world "worship" the dragon that gave life and authority to the composite beast, and then they "worship" the composite beast. The world is seen worshipping these two representatives of Babylon.

What is the relationship of the composite beast with the red dragon beast of Revelation 12? We already know from verse 2 that the dragon beast gave the composite beast power, seat, and authority. We know that this occurred in AD 538. This composite beast reigned 1,260 years until 1798 when it received a mortal wound. But verse 3 tells us that this composite beast received healing after 1798. The Weymouth translation of Revelation 13:4 tells us why.

And they offered worship to the Dragon, because it was to him that the Wild Beast owed his dominion; and they also offered worship to the Wild Beast, and said, "Who is there like him? And who is able to engage in battle with him?" (Rev. 13:4, Weymouth).

It was "to him [the dragon beast] that the Wild Beast [the composite beast] owed his dominion." The dragon beast is giving world class power or "dominion" to the composite beast for the second time. John tells us that the people of the world recognize the power of the dragon beast by worshipping him. But John tells us that they also recognize the power of the composite beast by worshipping him. What is going on here?

The people of the world "offered worship" to these two "wild beasts." We know that these two beasts are "world powers." What is it that we need to understand about this act of worship? The *Free Dictionary* tells us that worship means "reverent love and devotion accorded a deity, an idol, or a sacred object." They have given their hearts and souls to these two beasts. The point here is simple. The world is offering "reverent love and devotion" to "world powers" instead of to God. This type of worship is paganism.

Jesus combated such false worship when He responded to Satan's third temptation. He said: "Get thee hence, Satan: for it is written, Thou shalt worship the Lord thy God, and him only shalt thou serve" (Matt. 4:10). Worship belongs to God, not to idols. Then Jesus tells us that if you worship idols you will serve them.

The people of the world are aware of what John has described in the vision because they are part of what is happening. They are watching the red dragon heal the composite beast. They know that they are witnessing something extraordinary. The healing of the beast must point to great spiritual power.

As you think about worldly events and the world powers behind them, have you seen the "dragon" healing or restoring power to papal Rome in the last few years? The full restoration of the head of the composite beast by the dragon is still future. That means that this composite beast, though still around, is not as dominant a power today as it was years ago. Yet, John says that it will rise from its deathbed and will influence the destiny of the world. He further says that "the dragon" is the power that will give the composite beast this second chance and that the people of the world will worship "the dragon which gave power unto the beast" (Rev. 13:4).

Can you believe these words? The text tells us that we know that the world is watching the reappearance of the dragon. If pagan Rome, the dragon beast, was destroyed around AD 538, and if the composite beast reigned from AD 538 until 1798 when it received the mortal wound, and if the dragon beast revives the composite beast by healing its head after 1798, we must ask the next question. Have we seen this? Has this momentous and pivotal event occurred yet? It is my opinion that we have not yet seen this fulfillment. The next question is, what does this dragon beast represent in Revelation 13:4?

We know from the definitions of Revelation 12 that the dragon was symbolic of pagan Rome and Satan. So the question then becomes, is this dragon in Revelation 13:4, a symbol of the reappearance of pagan Rome or is Satan appearing as an angel of light for the third time to heal papal Rome?

This is a very important prophetic point. I believe that this dragon beast is no longer hiding. It will be seen by the world. That means that this dragon beast was, and is not, then is. This dragon beast is showing the world its power and influence, and the world reacts to this healing miracle. The world will not just give praise to the dragon beast and go on with life as usual. We are told that they will worship the dragon beast for what it has done for the composite beast. We are discussing the last major turning point for the people of the world. The world worships the dragon because they are in awe of the dragon. They are displaying their affections for the dragon. They are ready to follow the dragon in obedience. This action of the world worshipping the dragon is end-time prophecy. Are you ready for this worldwide event?

Let's consider another aspect of pagan Rome. When we think about the religion of pagan Rome, we realize that there is another important principle we need to consider. The religion of pagan Rome was and is spiritualism, which means that they lifted up idol worship or worship of manmade objects. Their main doctrine is that they believe in the idea of the immortality of the soul. So when John tells us that in Revelation 13:4 the world will worship the dragon, John seems to be saying that the world will be worshipping the king of spiritualism.

Daniel 12:11 tells us that "from the time that the daily *sacrifice* shall be taken away, and the abomination that maketh desolate set up, there shall be a thousand two hundred and ninety days." The daily, the pagan system of Satan, will be replaced with the new system. The seven-headed idol seen with the dragon, the composite beast, and the image to the beast will be replaced with the real beast: the eighth beast. In this book, I will show how the seven-headed image that is seen with the dragon beast will be replaced by the real beast: the eighth beast. The world will not worship the old serpent, nor the angel-like being that stood before Jesus. They will worship a being that will look just like and sound just like Jesus Christ. All their senses will be overwhelmed. They will be captivated and taken captive by this *anti*christ, which means "one who takes the place of Christ." The appearance of Satan as Christ, Ellen White points out, will occur after the establishment of the "image to the beast" and the close of probation (see *Spirit of Prophecy*, vol. 4, p. 440 and *The Great Controversy*, p. 614).

> As the crowning act in the great drama of deception, Satan himself will personate Christ. The church has long professed to look to the Saviour's advent as the consummation of her hopes. Now the great deceiver will make it appear that Christ has come. In different parts of the earth, Satan will manifest himself among men as a majestic being of dazzling brightness, resembling the description of the Son of God given by John in the Revelation. Revelation 1:13–15. The glory that surrounds him is unsurpassed by anything that mortal eyes have yet beheld. The shout of triumph rings out upon the air: "Christ has come! Christ has come!" The people prostrate themselves in adoration before him, while he lifts up his hands and pronounces a blessing upon them, as Christ blessed His disciples when He was upon the earth. His voice is soft and subdued, yet full of melody. In gentle, compassionate tones he presents some of the same gracious, heavenly truths which the Saviour uttered; he heals the diseases of the people, and then, in his assumed character of Christ, he claims to have changed the Sabbath to Sunday, and commands all to hallow the day which he has blessed. He declares that those who persist in keeping holy the seventh day are blaspheming his name by refusing to listen to his angels sent to them with light and truth. This is the strong, almost overmastering delusion. Like the Samaritans who were deceived by Simon Magus, the multitudes, from the least to the greatest, give heed to these sorceries, saying: This is "the great power of God." Acts 8:10. (Ellen G. White, *The Great Controversy*, p. 624)

What else does John describe? "And they worshipped the dragon which gave power unto the beast: and they worshipped the beast, saying, Who is like unto the beast? who is able to make war with him?" (Rev. 13:4). Why do they worship the dragon? They recognize that it is the dragon that gives power or authority to the composite beast. Then they say, "Who is stronger or mightier then the [composite] beast that we worship? Who would dare stand against him?"

What does John say will happen next? What is the future influence of the beast?

> And there was given unto him a mouth speaking great things and blasphemies; and power was given unto him to continue forty and two months. And he opened his mouth in blasphemy against God, to blaspheme his name, and his tabernacle, and them that dwell in heaven. And it was given unto him to make war with the saints, and to overcome them: and power was given him over all kindreds, and tongues, and nations. And all that dwell upon the earth shall worship him, whose names are not written in the book of life of the Lamb slain from the foundation of the world. (Rev. 13:5–8)

John tells us that "he" is given mighty powers. Who is this "he"? We know that the dragon is a symbol of Satan, pagan Rome, and spiritualism. We know that the composite beast is papal Rome. We know that both of them will be worshipped by the world at the same time. Who then is the "he" of verses 5 to 8?

Let's figure it out. We were told that the composite beast of Revelation 13 received "his power, and his seat, and great authority" (Rev. 13:2) from the dragon the first time. So it would be logical that the composite beast is given a second chance to have power or authority as a kingdom. This composite beast will be given a mouth to speak blasphemies against God, the temple of God, and the people of God. Then John tells us that this composite beast is given authority for a specific time: forty-two months. Finally, this beast comes to the point when he makes war against the saints.

Each of these points is important. Blaspheming is showing contempt and disrespect for God with your words or actions. This beast goes beyond that. John tells us that this beast shows contempt and disrespect for God, for the foundation of His government, and the people that God calls His own. How can this beast blaspheme these things? This beast has made up its own religion. They have removed God and placed themselves in the seat of God. They have made changes to the law of God that point to themselves and not God. They have replaced the man of faith with the man of works. They have developed a system of religion that is based on power and force and not on the freedom to choose.

Secondly, we are given a specific time that this beast will triumph: forty-two months or 1,260 days, or three and a half years. This is the time that God has allotted to this false system. But what is interesting is that we will find that is the same time period that God has given to His followers to warn His people of the second coming in Revelation 11.

Lastly, we are told that this beast will declare war against the saints of God. How is it that this composite beast is so frustrated by the saints of God that it lashes out against them and kills them? Remember Revelation 12:17? John is telling us that the dragon (Rev. 12:17) and the composite beast (Rev. 13:7) will declare war against the people of God because of anger over religious issues.

Then John tells us the next step that the world will take. They will give this supreme being, the dragon beast, power or authority over the world. This being will be worshipped by the whole world. Then John tells us the character of these followers. Those who worship this being will not have their names written in the Lamb's book of life. He is saying that those who worship the beast and his image will not go to heaven with Jesus at His second coming.

So, what have we learned so far? The composite beast will become a world power again, after it had received a mortal wound. It will stand next to the dragon. Both the composite beast and the dragon will receive the worship of the world. But the reign of the dragon and the composite beast will not be long.

Let's read some comments from *The Bible Knowledge Commentary*:

> 13:4–6. The supernatural character of *the beast* makes him the object of worship along with Satan, the source of his power. It has always been Satan's purpose to receive the worship due to God alone, as stated in Isaiah 14:14: "I will make myself like the Most High." This is Satan's final form of counterfeit religion in which he assumes the place of God the Father, and the beast or the world ruler assumes the role of King of kings as a substitute for Christ....
>
> Recognizing the supernatural character of Satan and the ruler, the question is raised, *Who is like the beast? Who can make war against him?* (Rev. 13:4) This apparently explains how the beast could become world ruler without a war. His blasphemous assumption of the role of God continues *for 42 months*, during which time he blasphemes *God* as well as heaven and *those who live in heaven*. (John F. Walvoord, *The Bible Knowledge Commentary: An Exposition of the Scriptures by Dallas Seminary Faculty*, Roy B. Zuck, ed., vol. 1 [Colorado Springs, CO: David C. Cook, 1983], pp. 960, 961, emphasis supplied)

This quotation tells us that the authors of *The Bible Knowledge Commentary* believe that Satan will assume the role of God the Father. It tells us that "papal Rome" will be given the role of the Son of man. But this vision given John in Revelation 13 does not stop with Satan and his role as God the Father. So let's continue. What does John tell us about the next beast or the second beast of Revelation 13?

The Beast with Two Lamblike Horns, Which Comes Out of the Earth

"And I beheld another beast coming up out of the earth; and he had two horns like a lamb, and he spake as a dragon. And he exerciseth all the power of the first beast before him, and causeth the earth and them which dwell therein to worship the first beast, whose deadly wound was healed" (Rev. 13:11, 12).

Another beast arrives on the scene. John tells us that this second beast of Revelation 13 looks like a lamb with two horns, but its character is revealed with its voice. It speaks like the beast of Revelation 12, the dragon—this second beast has the voice of the dragon. How did the dragon of Revelation 12 (pagan

Rome) fulfill the goals of its government? It was by force. It was their way or death. This second beast in Revelation 13 is said to "exerciseth all the power of the first beast before him," which is telling us that this lamblike beast is following in the steps of the dragon beast and is using force to accomplish its goals. This lamblike beast will use force to make the world worship the beast that had the wounded head (the composite beast).

We believe that the beast with the wounded head is papal Rome. John is telling us that this second beast forces the world to worship papal Rome. We know that one of the foundational principles of papal Rome is their self-declaration that they were given the right to change the law of God. This "manmade" right was exercised when the fundamental law of the Sabbath was changed 1,500 years ago by this church. They declared that Sunday instead of the Sabbath should be the day of worship. So, when this second beast forces the world to worship the first beast, we believe that this false doctrine, Sunday sacredness, will take center stage.

In other words, this verse is a prophecy of what will take place in the near future. We believe that the second beast of Revelation 13, symbol of the United States of America, will act like the dragon. It will pass a law and force its citizens to worship on a specific day for the good of the nation. This beast will pass a law that will state that Sunday will be the official recognized day of worship within its boundaries. At first the people of this great nation will be led to think that this law will help stabilize some great physical or spiritual problem, but then this beast will pass laws that will give this Sunday law teeth to force its citizens to comply with the new law. But the narrative does not end with the Sunday law. The next verses describe the coming out of another beast:

> And he doeth great wonders, so that he maketh fire come down from heaven on the earth in the sight of men, And deceiveth them that dwell on the earth by the means of those miracles which he had power to do in the sight of the beast; saying to them that dwell on the earth, that they should make an image to the beast, which had the wound by a sword, and did live. (Rev. 13:13, 14)

What is this great wonder? Fire will be called down from heaven during the reign of the lamblike beast of Revelation 13. John tells us that this great wonder will deceive the people of the earth. Then this beast will call for the formation of a new world government. They will refer to this new government as the "image to the beast." This new government will look very much like the dragon beast and the composite beast of Revelation 13. Who is this creature that is asking for the creation of a new government? Ellen G. White gives us an answer:

In Revelation we read concerning Satan: "And he doeth great wonders, so that he maketh fire come down from heaven on the earth in the sight of men, and deceiveth them that dwell on the earth by the means of those miracles which he had power to do in the sight of the beast; saying to them that dwell on the earth, that they should make an image to the beast, which had the wound by a sword, and did live. And he had power to give life unto the image of the beast, that the image of the beast should both speak, and cause that as many as would not worship the image of the beast should be killed. And he causeth all, both small and great, rich and poor, free and bond, to receive a mark in their right hand, or in their foreheads: and that no man might buy or sell, save he that had the mark, or the name of the beast, or the number of his name" (Revelation 13:13-17). (*Selected Messages*, bk. 3, p. 393)

Ellen White tells us that it is Satan who "maketh fire come down from heaven on the earth in the sight of men." We know him. He was the beast that was seen ready to devour the baby Jesus. He was the same dragon beast that was seen healing the wound of the composite beast. And now we are told that he will be working alongside the lamblike beast by causing fire to come down from heaven. But the biblical text does not stop there. It says that this beast will deceive all who "dwell on the earth by the means of those miracles which he had power to do in the sight of the beast." The text states that this dragon will have an international, worldwide influence. Then this dragon will issue an order. He will command them "that dwell on the earth, that they should make an image to the beast, which had the wound by a sword, and did live."

The dragon (a.k.a. Satan) gave power to the composite beast or papal Rome in Revelation 13:2, and again in Revelation 13:4 he revives the composite beast from the mortal wound. But here in Revelation 13:14 John tells us that he is giving power to another world power—this one is called "the image of the beast." This "image of the beast" is the next beast or the third beast of Revelation 13. What kind of power does this dragon have? He will have enough power to "give life unto the image of the beast, that the image of the beast should both speak, and cause that as many as would not worship the image of the beast should be killed." This dragon beast has the power to give life to another world power. This last world power, the "image to the beast," the new world order, will pass a death decree. What does this new third world power of Revelation 13 demand? Worship the religion of the new world order or be killed.

Does this new information make this chapter come alive? John was given these visions that we might understand the evil force that is behind the scenes of Revelation 12. The red dragon first is introduced, but we know that it is a representation of Satan. Here in Revelation 13 we see him standing before the world being worshipped with the composite beast at the time of the end; then he is seen bringing down fire from heaven with the lamblike beast at the time of the end; then we see him directing the formation of a new world order, known as the image of the beast, at the time of the end. Is Satan working with three different power or is it actually one religious power at the time of the end? What we know for sure is that Satan was seen tempting Christ, then he seems to disappear, then we see him at the time of the end working with worldly powers. We can say that this dragon that was seen, then not seen, then seen again is Satan.

Who are these world powers that we have described in Revelation 12 and 13? They are the enemies of God. Let's read about them:

> Under the symbols of a great red dragon, a leopard-like beast, and a beast with lamblike horns, the earthly governments which would especially engage in trampling

upon God's law and persecuting His people, were presented to John. The war is carried on till the close of time. The people of God, symbolized by a holy woman and her children, were represented as greatly in the minority. In the last days only a remnant still existed. Of these John speaks as they "which keep the commandments of God, and have the testimony of Jesus Christ" (Rev. 12:17). (Ellen G. White, *Signs of the Times*, Nov. 1, 1899)

The statements of this author are very clear. The great red dragon (Rev. 12:3), the leopard-like beast (Rev. 13:1, 2), and the lamblike beast (Rev. 13:11) are earthly governments that trample on God's law and persecute His people. She states that this action against the church of Christ is "war." This "war" will continue "till the close of time." In the next paragraph, this author tells us who she thinks they are:

Through paganism, and then through the Papacy, Satan exerted his power for many centuries in an effort to blot from the earth God's faithful witnesses. Pagans and papists were actuated by the same dragon spirit. They differed only in that the Papacy, making a pretense of serving God, was the more dangerous and cruel foe. Through the agency of Romanism, Satan took the world captive. The professed church of God was swept into the ranks of this delusion, and for more than a thousand years the people of God suffered under the dragon's ire. And when the Papacy, robbed of its strength, was forced to desist from persecution, John beheld a new power coming up to echo the dragon's voice, and carry forward the same cruel and blasphemous work. This power, the last that is to wage war against the church and the law of God, was symbolized by a beast with lamblike horns. The beasts preceding it had risen from the sea, but this came up out of the earth, representing the peaceful rise of the nation which is symbolized. The "two horns like a lamb" well represent the character of the United States Government.... (*Signs of the Times*, Nov. 1, 1899)

She states that through pagan Rome and then through papal Rome, Satan tried to destroy God's family. Then she tells us that the United States of America will become the next power to wage war against the church and the law of God. Who is behind these political powers? The answer is in the first sentence of the above quote: "Through paganism, and then through the Papacy, Satan exerted his power for many centuries in an effort to blot from the earth God's faithful witnesses."

We read that Satan is the beast that is behind the Roman power of paganism that tried to destroy the people of God during the time that Jesus walked on the earth. He is the beast that is behind the papal power that tried to destroy the people of God during the 1,260 years of its dominion. He will be the one who will influence the United States government of the apostate Protestants that will try to destroy the power of God. We see three beasts and their works, but behind them is the great red dragon. Who are these beasts that act a part in Satan's plan for the time of the end? Let's diagram them:

- The great red dragon — Paganism (spiritualism) of Rome
- The leopard-like beast — Papal Rome
- The beast with the lamblike horns — United States of America

What do these three kingdoms have to do with one another? Let's look at another statement of Ellen G. White:

Through the two great errors, the immortality of the soul and Sunday sacredness, Satan will bring the people under his deceptions. While the former lays the foundation of Spiritualism, the latter creates a bond of sympathy with Rome. The Protestants of the United States will be foremost in stretching their hands across the gulf to grasp the hand of Spiritualism; they will reach over the abyss to clasp hands with the Roman power; and under the influence of this threefold union, this country will follow in the steps of Rome in trampling on the rights of conscience. (*The Great Controversy*, p. 588)

What are the three powers that will unite in the time of the end?
- The spiritualism of pagan Rome
- The Protestants of the United States
- The papal power

What was said about these three world powers? "…Under the influence of this threefold union, this country will follow in the steps of Rome in trampling on the rights of conscience."

Who will unite with Satan to make war against the church of Christ?
- Spiritualism: the religion of pagan Rome
- The lamblike power: the apostate Protestants of the United States
- The papists: papal Rome
- What will this three-fold union be called?

Our answer is found in Revelation 17. That chapter tell us that this spiritual union will be called Babylon. This three-fold union will unite with the next world power to prepare the world for the eighth king. Now you know why it says at the end of chapter 12 that the dragon (a.k.a. spiritualism) "will make war with the remnant of her seed" (Rev. 12:17). Why it says that the composite beast of papal Rome "will make war with the saints" (Rev. 13:7). And finally, why it says that the lamblike beast (a.k.a. the United States of America) will make war against those who will not worship the "image to the beast" (Rev. 13:15).

We are looking at the spiritual aspect of each of these world powers. The false doctrine of the immortality of the soul of spiritualistic pagan Rome, the error of Sunday sacredness of papal Rome, and the apostate actions of the Protestants of the United States will all unite that the new world order of Satan will take place. They will lead the world to a government that unites church and state, and they will "trample … on the rights of conscience."

Let's review the verse that we are focusing on at this time: "And he doeth great wonders, so that he maketh fire come down from heaven on the earth in the sight of men, and deceiveth them that dwell on the earth by the means of those miracles which he had power to do in the sight of the beast …" (Rev. 13:13, 14).

The cause of Babylon will take a giant leap forward when Satan brings down fire from heaven (Rev. 13:13). So let's take a look at this miracle of fire from heaven. We will being our study of this phenomenon with the last time that fire had come down from heaven.

> It is the hour of the evening sacrifice, and Elijah bids the people, "Come near unto me." As they tremblingly draw near, he turns to the broken-down altar where once men worshipped the God of heaven, and repairs it. To him this heap of ruins is more precious than all the magnificent altars of heathendom....
>
> The altar completed, the prophet makes a trench about it, and, having put the wood in order and prepared the bullock, he lays the victim on the altar and commands the people to flood the sacrifice and the altar with water. "Fill four barrels," he directed, "and pour it on the burnt sacrifice, and on the wood. And he said, Do it the second time. And they did it the second time. And he said, Do it the third time. And they did it the third time. And the water ran round about the altar; and he filled the trench also with water."
>
> Reminding the people of the long-continued apostasy that has awakened the wrath of Jehovah, Elijah calls upon them to humble their hearts and turn to the God of their fathers, that the curse upon the land of Israel may be removed. Then, bowing reverently before the unseen God, he raises his hands toward heaven and offers a simple prayer. Baal's priests have screamed and foamed and leaped, from early morning until late in the afternoon; but as Elijah prays, no senseless shrieks resound over Carmel's height. He prays as if he knows Jehovah is there, a witness to the scene, a listener to his appeal. The prophets of Baal have prayed wildly, incoherently. Elijah prays simply and fervently, asking God to show His superiority over Baal, that Israel may be led to turn to Him.
>
> "Lord God of Abraham, Isaac, and of Israel," the prophet pleads, "let it be known this day that Thou art God in Israel, and that I am Thy servant, and that I have done all these things at Thy word. Hear me, O Lord, hear me, that this people may know that Thou art the Lord God, and that Thou hast turned their heart back again." ...
>
> No sooner is the prayer of Elijah ended than flames of fire, like brilliant flashes of lightning, descend from heaven upon the upreared altar, consuming the sacrifice, licking up the water in the trench, and consuming even the stones of the altar. The brilliancy of the blaze illumines the mountain and dazzles the eyes of the multitude. In the valleys below, where many are watching in anxious suspense the movements of those above, the descent of fire is clearly seen, and all are amazed at the sight. It resembles the pillar of fire which at the Red Sea separated the children of Israel from the Egyptian host.
>
> The people on the mount prostrate themselves in awe before the unseen God. They dare not continue to look upon the Heaven-sent fire. They fear that they themselves will be consumed; and, convicted of their duty to acknowledge the God of Elijah as the

God of their fathers, to whom they owe allegiance, they cry out together as with one voice, "The Lord, He is the God; the Lord, He is the God." With startling distinctness the cry resounds over the mountain and echoes in the plain below. At last Israel is aroused, undeceived, penitent. At last the people see how greatly they have dishonored God. The character of Baal worship, in contrast with the reasonable service required by the true God, stands fully revealed. The people recognize God's justice and mercy in withholding the dew and the rain until they have been brought to confess His name. They are ready now to admit that the God of Elijah is above every idol. (*Prophets and Kings*, pp. 152, 153)

Elijah was a man who obeyed God. He obeyed God before the famine began by telling the king that the famine would last forty-two months. He obeyed on the mount and prayed for a sign that God was real. His prayer was answered. This act of fire was the first step of reform for Israel.

In Revelation 13 John tells us a different story about fire from heaven. He tells us that a beast will make "fire come down from heaven on the earth in the sight of men" (Rev. 13:13). This next fire from heaven will not be from the God in heaven, but it will come from the power of Satan. It will reveal to the world that this new beast, the dragon beast, has amazing and miraculous powers. What was the reaction of the people to the fire 2,500 years ago?

> The people on the mount prostrate themselves in awe before the unseen God. They dare not continue to look upon the Heaven-sent fire. They fear that they themselves will be consumed; and, convicted of their duty to acknowledge the God of Elijah as the God of their fathers, to whom they owe allegiance, they cry out together as with one voice, "The Lord, He is the God; the Lord, He is the God." … At last Israel is aroused, undeceived, penitent. (*Prophets and Kings*, p. 153)

We are told that the people of Israel were "aroused, undeceived, penitent." A new era of reform began in Israel.

What will happen to the world when a beast will make "fire come down from heaven on the earth in the sight of men" (Rev. 13:13)? They will be "aroused," but their reaction will be different. They will be "deceived" and "unpenitent" by this last beast.

So, if the prophets of Baal were slain on Mount Carmel by the true prophet of God, will the prophetic writings of the two witnesses, Daniel and John, be slain on the same mountain by the new beast in this future event? Because we are told, "And when they shall have finished their testimony, the beast that ascendeth out of the bottomless pit shall make war against them, and shall overcome them, and kill them" (Rev. 11:7). How can God allow such a display? How can He allow His word to be destroyed?

The words of Elijah are pertinent at this juncture: "How long halt ye between two opinions? if the Lord be God, follow him: but if [Satan], then follow him" (1 Kings 18:21).

There will be only two groups standing at the time of the end. You have seen the good guys in Revelation 4 to 11. God is not showing you the other guys in Revelation 12 and 13. What do these two groups look like?

> There are only two parties upon the earth—those who stand under the blood-stained banner of Jesus Christ and those who stand under the black banner of rebellion. Those who stand under Christ's banner bear the sign of obedience spoken of in Exodus 31:12–18 …
>
> Satan will work the miracles to deceive those who dwell upon the earth. Spiritualism will do its work by causing the dead to be personated. Those religious bodies who refuse to hear God's messages of warning will be under strong deception, and will unite with the civil power to persecute the saints. The Protestant churches will unite with the papal power in persecuting the commandment-keeping people of God. This is that power which constitutes the great system of persecution which will exercise spiritual tyranny over the consciences of men.
>
> "He had two horns like a lamb, and he spake as a dragon." Though professing to be followers of the Lamb of God, men become imbued with the spirit of the dragon. They profess to be meek and humble but they speak and legislate with the spirit of Satan, showing by their actions that they are the opposite of what they profess to be. This lamblike power unites with the dragon in making war upon those who keep the commandments of God and have the testimony of Jesus Christ. And Satan unites with Protestants and papists, acting in consort with them as the god of this world, dictating to men as if they were the subjects of his kingdom, to be handled and governed and controlled as he pleases. (*Manuscript Releases*, vol. 14, p. 162)

There are only two parties standing on the earth at the time of the end. Spiritualism unites with apostate Protestantism and the papal power forming the great system of persecution.

Let's finish chapter 13 of Revelation. After the fire from heaven, John tells us that Satan will ask the reigning governments to unite and form a new world order.

> And he doeth great wonders, so that he maketh fire come down from heaven on the earth in the sight of men, and deceiveth them that dwell on the earth by the means of those miracles which he had power to do in the sight of the beast; saying to them that dwell on the earth, that they should make an image to the beast, which had the wound by a sword, and did live. (Rev. 13:13, 14)

Then John tells us what happens:

> And he had power to give life unto the image of the beast, that the image of the beast should both speak, and cause that as many as would not worship the image of the beast should be killed. And he causeth all, both small and great, rich and poor, free and bond, to receive a mark in their right hand, or in their foreheads: And that no man might buy or sell, save he that had the mark, or the name of the beast, or the number of his name. (Rev. 13:15–17)

The dragon beast that is working through the lamblike beast gives life to the third beast of Revelation 13. This last beast of Revelation 13 is called "the image of the beast." This "image to the beast" will speak like the dragon that made it. The "image" will declare that those who worship "the image of the beast" will receive a mark in their right hand or in their forehead. This beast will also declare that those who refuse to worship "the image of the beast" will die. This is the death decree. Receive the mark of "the beast" or die.

> If men will not agree to trample under foot the commandments of God, the spirit of the dragon is revealed. They are imprisoned, brought before councils, and fined. "He causeth all, both small and great, rich and poor, free and bond, to receive a mark in their right hand, or in their foreheads" [Revelation 13:16]. "He had power to give life unto the image of the beast, that the image of the beast should both speak, and cause that as many as would not worship the image of the beast should be killed" [verse 15]. *Thus Satan usurps the prerogatives of Jehovah. The man of sin sits in the seat of God, proclaiming himself to be God, and acting above God.* (*Manuscript Releases*, vol. 14, p. 162, emphasis supplied)

Where is Satan doing these things? John tells us. He is sitting in the seat of God. Where on earth is the seat of God? Would it not be in the holy city of Jerusalem in the temple of God? God might look defeated at this point, but the rest of the story is found in Revelation 11 and 17.

> And when they shall have finished their testimony, the beast that ascendeth out of the bottomless pit shall make war against them, and shall overcome them, and kill them. And their dead bodies shall lie in the street of the great city, which spiritually is called Sodom and Egypt, where also our Lord was crucified. And they of the people and kindreds and tongues and nations shall see their dead bodies three days and an half, and shall not suffer their dead bodies to be put in graves. And they that dwell upon the earth shall rejoice over them, and make merry, and shall send gifts one to another; because these two prophets tormented them that dwelt on the earth. And after three days and an half the Spirit of life from God entered into them, and they stood upon their feet; and great fear fell upon them which saw them. And they heard a great voice

from heaven saying unto them, Come up hither. And they ascended up to heaven in a cloud; and their enemies beheld them. (Rev. 11:7–12)

When the prophets, Daniel and John, come to the end of the 1,260 days of their prophecy, the devil, the one that will arise from the pit, will come against them and kill them. As you have read in the text above, this action will be seen by the whole world. This is the death decree from Revelation 13: this death decree will be carried out by the dragon.

This incredible act will deceive many. The world will think that this new beast is God and that he has re-written His word. They will worship him. They will make him their king. Then John gives us the identification number of this beast.

Here is wisdom. Let him that hath understanding count the number of the beast: for it is the number of a man; and his number is Six hundred threescore and six. (Rev. 13:18)

The number for the beast and the number for his followers will be the same. It is the number 666. Right now that number does not give us any clue as to the followers of Satan, but we will discuss this shortly.

We have studied the events of Revelation 12 and 13 and discovered that God is revealing the last-day events of the enemy of God. This dragon beast sinned against God and developed his own system of religion. Revelation 12 and 13 is a study of the idol that Satan has created. He concocted a false religious system to lead the people of the earth from the worship of the true God. Let's read Revelation 17 and learn more about this false religious system.

> Thank you, Father, for the amazing details of the plan of Satan. I feel overwhelmed like the soldiers of Saul before the giant Goliath. But unlike them, I have Your Word. "The Lord will fight for you, and you shall hold your peace." Help me, Lord, to trust in You and Your Word. Amen.

Chapter 5
An Unholy Union

God has warned us that we will come face to face with His enemy at the time of the end. Revelation 12 and 13 describe the great red dragon, the composite beast, the two-horned beast, and the image of the beast. We found that with a quotation from Ellen G. White that the red dragon, the composite beast, and the two-horned beast will form a spiritual union that will be known as the "great system of persecution which will exercise spiritual tyranny over the consciences of men" (*Manuscript Releases*, vol. 14, p. 161).

Revelation chapter 17 gives us more details about this religious power and how its agenda will be implemented. We read: "And there came one of the seven angels which had the seven vials, and talked with me, saying unto me, Come hither; I will show unto thee the judgment of the great whore that sitteth upon many waters" (Rev. 17:1).

An angel next to the throne of God invites John to consider an event that will occur at the time of the end. He says, *Come with me so I can show you something you need to see. It is the judgment of the prostitute who sits on many waters.* John has not been given any information about this prostitute in previous visions. He doesn't understand the angel, but like us, he knows that this vision is important.

A prostitute is a woman who has intimate relations with men for money. She has no legal rights in this relationship. She prostitutes herself for monetary gain and not for love. It is her ambition to take care of herself and not the one that she is with. The angel tells us two things about the prostitute in Revelation 17. She is about to be judged by the God of heaven for the actions revealed in the vision. The second fact is that she is sitting on many waters.

> With whom the kings of the earth have committed fornication, and the inhabitants of the earth have been made drunk with the wine of her fornication. (Rev. 17:2)

The angel tells us that this prostitute has had immoral relationships with the kings of the earth and that she has made the inhabitants of the earth drunk with the wine of her fornication.

From this description, we recognize that this woman is not a virtuous woman. She dresses to stimulate the senses. She flatters the pride of her customers. She uses wine to weaken their ability to think. She gives that she might take for herself. She prostitutes her love to gain money and influence. She lives for her desires and her needs and her goals, for herself and not for her partners. She looks desirable, but her way is the way of death. Solomon was right. "There is a way which seemeth right unto a man, but the end thereof *are* the ways of death" (Prov. 14:12).

The angel tells us that she has given herself to the kings of the earth in an unholy union. These deluded kings join her in the doctrines of falsehood, because they are without reason and without conscience.

This prostitute has made the inhabitants of the earth drunk with her false doctrine. They are wasted in this drunkenness and unable to discern between good and evil. They are not capable of intelligent choices.

As we think about the angel's declarations, we realize that the events he describes are universal and that they have not yet happened because the angel is prophesying about the time of the end. What we must understand is that heaven is describing the result of a relationship between a religious system and the political world.

The Bible Knowledge Commentary summarizes what these two verses are saying:

> 17:1, 2. One of the seven angels (in chap. 16) who had one of the seven bowls invited John to witness the punishment of the great prostitute, who sits on many waters. This evil woman symbolizes the religious system of Babylon, and the waters symbolize "peoples, multitudes, nations, and languages" (v. 15). The angel informed John that the kings of the earth had committed adultery with the woman; in other words, they had become a part of the religious system which she symbolized (cf. 14:8). (*The Bible Knowledge Commentary: An Exposition of the Scriptures by Dallas Seminary Faculty*, vol. 1, p. 970)

The union of the woman and the beast symbolize the union of church and state. They have joined together for a common goal. What other details does God want us to understand about this unholy union? "So he carried me away in the spirit into the wilderness: and I saw a woman sit upon a scarlet coloured beast, full of names of blasphemy, having seven heads and ten horns" (Rev. 17:3).

The first two verses provide an overview of the vision. In verse 3, John sees the prostitute sitting on a scarlet beast and tells us that the name of the beast is "blasphemy." That it is "blasphemy" means that the beast claims for itself the attributes and rights of God. Besides describing the beast as having seven heads and ten horns, John says about the prostitute: "And the woman was arrayed in purple and scarlet colour, and decked with gold and precious stones and pearls, having a golden cup in her hand full of abominations and filthiness of her fornication" (Rev. 17:4).

John tells us that this woman is dressed in the royal colors of purple and scarlet. She is adorned with jewelry of gold, pearls and precious stones. Then John points his finger to the danger of this false religious organization. She has a golden cup filled with wine in her right hand. What we are not told is that this wine has been dedicated to the idol that Satan presents to the world. John identifies the wine in the cup as "full of abominations and filthiness of her fornication." Ellen White describes the wine in the cup:

> … Babylon has been fostering poisonous doctrines, the wine of error. This wine of error is made up of false doctrines, such as the natural immortality of the soul, the

eternal torment of the wicked, the denial of the pre-existence of Christ prior to his birth in Bethlehem, and advocating and exalting the first day of the week above God's holy, sanctified day .... (*Review and Herald*, Sept. 12, 1893)

This prostitute has sold her soul to the devil. She is riding the beast and is telling us to drink the wine and join the majority who worship the idol of the enemy of God and ultimately Satan himself. "And upon her forehead was a name written, MYSTERY, BABYLON THE GREAT, THE MOTHER OF HARLOTS AND ABOMINATIONS OF THE EARTH" (Rev. 17:5). "Babylon" is the prostitute's name. Her character is seen on her forehead. She has not only given herself to harlotry, but she has led others into the profession.

> … she exerts a corrupting influence upon the world by teaching doctrines which are opposed to the plainest statements of Holy Writ. (*The Great Controversy*, p. 388)

> … If we turn from the testimony of God's word, and accept false doctrines because our fathers taught them, we fall under the condemnation pronounced upon Babylon; we are drinking of the wine of her abomination. (*The Great Controversy*, p. 536)

John reveals what this false religious system will do. "And I saw the woman drunken with the blood of the saints, and with the blood of the martyrs of Jesus: and when I saw her, I wondered with great admiration" (Rev. 17:6).

John tells us that he saw the woman sit on the beast with seven heads and ten horns. Then, he tells us that the woman was drunken with the blood of innocent victims. The victims are those who know God and are carrying the warning message to the world. "Babylon the great" is a persecutor of the followers of the church of Christ. She has already spilled the blood of many saints of God and of the witnesses of Jesus. John cannot believe what he is seeing. He says that he was in shock. John's reaction is understandable. We ask ourselves the same question: How can a religious system, which believes it has the truth, kill the followers of the true God who have been sent out as witnesses of His prophecies? Is this not akin to the question we ask after reading the account of Jesus on the cross: How could the professed people of God kill the Messiah—the Lamb of God?

> And the angel said unto me, Wherefore didst thou marvel? I will tell thee the mystery of the woman, and of the beast that carrieth her, which hath the seven heads and ten horns. (Rev. 17:7)

The reaction of John to the vision of Babylon does not go unnoticed. The angel's question implies: *Why are you concerned with the form and the actions of the prostitute, when you should be warning the world about her false doctrines? Beware! She is a wolf in sheep's clothing.* Then the angel tells John that he is about to identify the woman on the beast so that he can pass it on to those living at the time of the end.

The angel begins with the description of the beast. He says that this scarlet-colored beast has seven heads and ten horns. Why should he reveal the number of its heads and horns? It is helpful as we compare it to other descriptions in Revelation that list the number of heads and horns of various creatures. The first is in Revelation 12:3, which describes the great red dragon: "And there appeared another wonder in heaven; and behold a great red dragon, having *seven heads* and *ten horns*, and seven crowns upon his heads" (Rev. 12:3, emphasis supplied). We have learned that this red dragon is a symbol of Satan and pagan Rome (Rev. 12:9).

The next description is in Revelation 13:1: "And I stood upon the sand of the sea, and saw a beast rise up out of the sea, having *seven heads* and *ten horns*, and upon his horns ten crowns, and upon his heads the name of blasphemy" (emphasis supplied). Revelation 13:1 describes the composite beast. This beast represents papal Rome.

The crowns are what distinguish the descriptions of pagan Rome and papal Rome. The dragon has a crown for each of its seven heads while the beast has a crown for each of its ten horns. The next beast with horns is found in Revelation 13:11. "And I beheld another beast coming up out of the earth; and he had *two horns* like a lamb, and he spake as a dragon." No crowns are mentioned. We can compare these three beasts in a diagram:

Dragon	7 heads	10 horns	7 crowns for 7 heads
Leopard-like Beast	7 heads	10 horns	10 crowns for 10 horns
Lamblike Beast	1 head	2 horns	no crowns

The next symbol with numerous heads and horns would be the image to the beast in Revelation 13:14: "And deceiveth them that dwell on the earth by the means of those miracles which he had power to do in the sight of the beast; saying to them that dwell on the earth, that they should make an image to the beast, which had the wound by a sword, and did live" (Rev. 13:14). The beast with the lamblike horns commands the world to make an image to the composite beast. This means that it will resemble the composite beast. What are the physical characteristics of the composite beast? The composite beast has seven heads, ten horns, and ten crowns for the ten horns. It is therefore possible that the image to the beast likewise has seven heads and ten horns. How many crowns will the image to the beast have? Revelation 13 does not mention any. Here is a summary of all the beasts we have studied.

Pagan Rome	7 heads	10 horns	7 crowns for 7 heads
Papal Rome	7 heads	10 horns	10 crowns for 10 horns
Lamblike Beast	1 head	2 horns	no crowns
Image to the Beast	7 heads	10 horns	no crowns

Moving on to chapter 17, how does John describe the beast in this chapter?

> And the angel said unto me, Wherefore didst thou marvel? I will tell thee the mystery of the woman, and of the beast that carrieth her, which hath the seven heads and ten horns. (Rev. 17:7)

The beast that carries the woman with "Babylon the Great" on her forehead has seven heads and ten horns. How many crowns does the beast have? The text does not mention any. We can add the image to the beast and the beast that carries the woman to our list:

Pagan Rome	7 heads	10 horns	7 crowns for 7 heads
Papal Rome	7 heads	10 horns	10 crowns for 10 horns
Lamblike Beast	1 head	2 horns	no crowns
Image to the Beast	7 heads	10 horns	no crowns
Revelation 17 Beast	7 heads	10 horns	no crowns

Notice that, so far, the physical characteristics of the image to the beast of Revelation 13 and of the beast of Revelation 17 are the same. As we continue reading, we discover that, eventually, the beast of Revelation 17 does get crowns. Verse 12 tells us that "the ten horns which thou sawest are ten kings, which have received no kingdom as yet; but receive power as kings one hour with the beast" (Rev. 17:12). When a person receives power or authority as a king, he receives a crown. Thus, the beast carrying the woman will receive ten crowns for its ten horns when it reigns for one hour at the time of the end. We can add these crowns to our list.

Pagan Rome	7 heads	10 horns	7 crowns for 7 heads
Papal Rome	7 heads	10 horns	10 crowns for 10 horns
Lamblike Beast	1 head	2 horns	no crowns
Image to the Beast	7 heads	10 horns	no crowns
Revelation 17 Beast	7 heads	10 horns	10 crowns for 10 horns

This list makes the next observation easy. The beast of Revelation 17 looks just like the image to the beast of Revelation 13 before the crowns were added (Rev. 17:12). They both had seven heads, ten horns, and no crowns. Therefore, I believe that we can say that the image to the beast in Revelation 13 is the same beast that will carry Babylon in Revelation 17. The history of the image to the beast in Revelation 13 is magnified by the history of the beast that will carry Babylon in Revelation 17.

The image to the beast in Revelation 13 is the last kingdom developed by Satan. This prophecy is about to happen. We are near this time—the time of the end. I believe that, at that time of the end, it will receive ten crowns for the ten horns from the dragon-like beast. This description of this seven-headed and ten-horned beast in Revelation 17 is the "rest of the story" of the image to the beast in Revelation 13.

But that is not the end of this vision in Revelation 17. Let's go on.

> The beast that thou sawest was, and is not; and shall ascend out of the bottomless pit, and go into perdition: and they that dwell on the earth shall wonder, whose names were not written in the book of life from the foundation of the world, when they behold the beast that was, and is not, and yet is. (Rev. 17:8)

John gives us another clue about this beast of Revelation 17. This last beast has been seen but is not seen now. Then he gives us a prophecy that will occur when Jesus comes the third time to the earth. He tells us that this last beast will ascend out of a specific place. That place is called the bottomless pit. When this beast ascends out of this pit, it will then go into perdition. This last action of this beast will cause those who are *not* written in the book of life to wonder. Then he gives us an additional riddle. This beast is the beast that was seen in a previous vision, then was not seen, but will be seen in the future.

These future events are described in Revelation 20:

> And I saw an angel come down from heaven, having the key of the bottomless pit and a great chain in his hand. And he laid hold on the dragon, that old serpent, which is the Devil, and Satan, and bound him a thousand years, and cast him into the bottomless pit, and shut him up, and set a seal upon him, that he should deceive the nations no more, till the thousand years should be fulfilled: and after that he must be loosed a little season. (Rev. 20:1–3)

These verses tell us that Satan will be shut up in the "bottomless pit" by an angel with a key for 1,000 years. He will not be seen. Then we are told what will happen next:

> And when the thousand years are expired, Satan shall be loosed out of his prison, And shall go out to deceive the nations which are in the four quarters of the earth, Gog and Magog, to gather them together to battle: the number of whom is as the sand of the sea. And they went up on the breadth of the earth, and compassed the camp of the saints about, and the beloved city: and fire came down from God out of heaven, and devoured them. And the devil that deceived them was cast into the lake of fire and brimstone, where the beast and the false prophet are, and shall be tormented day and night for ever and ever. (Rev. 20:7–10)

These verses tell us that when the 1,000 years have expired then Satan will be "yet is." He will "go out to deceive the nations" for the last battle on earth. Satan and his followers will surround the city of the New Jerusalem, but judgment will be executed, and Satan and all his followers will be cast into the lake of fire. Thus, the Scriptures will be fulfilled. The beast that "was, and is not" will be the beast that "was, and is not, and yet is."

The seven heads are called mountains. The angel is telling us that the mountains are symbolic of political world powers that support the prostitute. She has chosen to sell her soul to this world power and is sitting on and influencing the beast that will rule the world.

When we consider the beasts of Revelation 12 and 13, we remember that the red dragon had seven heads, that the composite beast had seven heads, and that the image to the beast had seven heads. So what is the relationship of the beasts of these chapters to the beast of Revelation 17? Let's look at verse 10:

> "And there are seven kings:
> five are fallen,
> and one is,
> and the other is not yet come;
> and when he cometh, he must continue a short space."

The angel then tells some interesting facts. There are seven kings. Five of them have already fallen, one of them is currently reigning, and a seventh has not appeared. Yet, when this seventh king comes, he will reign for only a short time. Who are these kings? Let's solve the puzzle.

Verse 10 says that "five are fallen." When and where did these kings come from? We can look for an answer in the book of Daniel, but we must first consider the fact that the book of Daniel is considered a prophecy and that the book of Revelation is considered a revelation. So where in the book of Revelation does it talk about seven kings? John tells us about four powers or four kings in Revelation 12 and 13 and how they are divided, but he does not identify them by name. So let's examine the book of Daniel. In Daniel chapter two, Nebuchadnezzar dreamed about an idol that represented the kingdoms of the world after Babylon. Daniel wrote that after the golden kingdom of Babylon would come kingdoms of silver, then brass, then iron, and then iron mixed with clay, but again we are not able to identify them by name. But in Daniel 7, God gave the prophet enough details about the five kingdoms so that we can identify each one.

> Daniel spake and said, I saw in my vision by night, and, behold, the four winds of the heaven strove upon the great sea. And four great beasts came up from the sea, diverse one from another. The first was like a lion, and had eagle's wings: I beheld till the wings thereof were plucked, and it was lifted up from the earth, and made stand upon the feet as a man, and a man's heart was given to it. And behold another beast, a second, like to a bear, and it raised up itself on one side, and it had three ribs in the mouth of it between the teeth of it: and they said thus unto it, Arise, devour much flesh. After this I beheld, and lo another, like a leopard, which had upon the back of it four wings of a fowl; the beast had also four heads; and dominion was given to it. After this I saw in the night visions, and behold a fourth beast, dreadful and terrible, and strong

exceedingly; and it had great iron teeth: it devoured and brake in pieces, and stamped the residue with the feet of it: and it was diverse from all the beasts that were before it; and it had ten horns. I considered the horns, and, behold, there came up among them another little horn, before whom there were three of the first horns plucked up by the roots: and, behold, in this horn were eyes like the eyes of man, and a mouth speaking great things. (Dan. 7:2–8)

Daniel saw: (1) a beast like a lion, (2) one like a bear, (3) another like a leopard, (4) a terrible creature, and (5) a little horn arising from the terrible creature.

Let's make another list that defines these creatures. We know from the historical background of Daniel and his placement in Babylon that the first king mentioned by Daniel is Babylon:

Thou, O king, art a king of kings: for the God of heaven hath given thee a kingdom, power, and strength, and glory. And wheresoever the children of men dwell, the beasts of the field and the fowls of the heaven hath he given into thine hand, and hath made thee ruler over them all. *Thou art this head of gold.* (Dan. 2:37, 38)

The head of gold was the first kingdom mentioned by Daniel when he was interpreting the vision of the king of Babylon. The first kingdom in Daniel's dream was represented by a lion, which aptly symbolizes the kingdom of Babylon. The remaining world powers, according to historians, are Medo-Persia, Greece, and Rome. The Roman power can be divided into its pagan and papal phases. Therefore, according to history, here are the five successive powers that God revealed to Daniel.

The Five Kingdoms Listed in Daniel 7

1	The Lion	=	Babylon
2	The Bear	=	Medo-Persia
3	The Leopard	=	Greece
4	The Terrible Creature	=	Pagan Rome
5	The Little Horn from the Creature	=	Papal Rome

These kingdoms have come and gone, but their influence remains. Consider Daniel's description of the demise of little horn power:

I beheld then because of the voice of the great words which the horn spake: I beheld even till the beast was slain, and his body destroyed, and given to the burning flame. As concerning the rest of the beasts, they had their dominion taken away: yet their lives were prolonged for a season and time. (Dan. 7:11, 12)

The angel told Daniel that the "little horn" will eventually end up in "the burning flame." Then he told him that "the lives" of "the rest of the beasts" will last for "a season and time." Who are the rest of the beasts Daniel is referring to? Revelation 13 provides clues:

> And I stood upon the sand of the sea, and saw a beast rise up out of the sea, having seven heads and ten horns, and upon his horns ten crowns, and upon his heads the name of blasphemy. And the beast which I saw was like unto a leopard, and his feet were as the feet of a bear, and his mouth as the mouth of a lion: and the dragon gave him his power, and his seat, and great authority. And I saw one of his heads as it were wounded to death; and his deadly wound was healed: and all the world wondered after the beast. (Rev. 13:1–3)

The presence of the features of the lion, bear, and leopard in the composite beast of Revelation 13 tells us that the influence of the kingdoms of Babylon, Medo-Persia, and Greece is present in the composite beast. From John's description of the composite beast, we have already concluded that it is papal Rome, which incorporated ideology and philosophy from the four kingdoms of Daniel. But we do not yet have a list of the seven kingdoms mentioned in Revelation 17. Perhaps we can find more by considering the information given in Revelation 12 and 13. The beast in Revelation 12 is the dragon, representing pagan Rome. The beasts in Revelation 13 are the composite beast, the lamblike beast, and the image to the beast. We have concluded that these four beast are representative of pagan Rome, papal Rome, the United States of America, and the new world order. We can diagram them as follows:

The Beasts of Revelation 12 and 13

The Red Dragon	=	Pagan Rome
The Composite Beast	=	Papal Rome
The Lamblike Beast	=	The United States of America
The Image to the Beast	=	New World Order

In the following diagram, we will align the beasts of Daniel 7 with the beasts in Revelation 12 and 13.

	Beasts from Daniel 7	
1	Lion	Babylon
2	Bear	Medo-Persia
3	Leopard	Greece
4	Dreaded Beast	Pagan Rome
5	Little Horn	Papal Rome

	Beasts from Revelation 12 and 13	
1	Red Dragon	Pagan Rome
2	Composite Beast	Papal Rome
3	Lamblike Beast	United States of America
4	Image to the Beast	New World Order

Do you see what I see? The fourth and fifth beasts from Daniel 7 align with the first and second beasts from Revelation 12 and 13. Combining and renumbering the lists, we get the following:

Beasts from Daniel 7 and Revelation 12 and 13

1st	Lion	Babylon
2nd	Bear	Medo-Persia
3rd	Leopard	Greece
4th	Dreaded Beast or Red Dragon	Pagan Rome
5th	Little Horn or Composite Beast	Papal Rome
6th	Lamblike Beast	United States of America
7th	Image to the Beast	New World Order

I would propose that these are the seven kingdoms of Revelation 17. Repeating the puzzle of Revelation 17:10, we read: "And there are seven kings: *five are fallen*, and *one is, and the other is not yet come*; and when he cometh, he must continue a short space." We can add another column to our chart with this identifying information.

Beasts from Daniel 7 and Revelation 12 and 13

1st	Lion: Babylon	Fallen
2nd	Bear: Medo-Persia	Fallen
3rd	Leopard: Greece	Fallen
4th	Dreaded Beast/Red Dragon: Pagan Rome	Fallen
5th	Little Horn/Composite Beast: Papal Rome	Fallen
6th	Lamblike Beast: The United States of America	One is
7th	Image to the Beast: New World Order	The other is not yet come!

If these seven kingdoms are in their proper order, then we can make some amazing conclusions. First, Revelation 12 and 13 are a prophecy of the kingdoms that will have an influence on the earth at the time of the end. Each of them are about to declare war on the children of God. Second, the United States of America is the kingdom of Revelation 17:10 that is now in power. Third, the next kingdom, the new world order, which is described in the last few verses of Revelation 13 and in the beast that carries the harlot of Revelation 17, is about to appear. Yet, the angel is not done yet. He lists an eighth king. "And the beast that was, and is not, even he is the eighth, and is of the seven, and goeth into perdition" (Rev. 17:11).

The angel tells us that after the seventh beast there will be an eighth. He tells us that this eighth beast is the same one mentioned in verse 8 of this chapter. This is the ultimate beast that the prostitute will sit on—remember, she is not married to any one beast. She uses them. This ultimate beast is the beast that will be wondered after by those whose names were not written in the book of life. This eighth beast is the last king in the line of God's enemies. I would assert that this eighth beast is none other than Satan himself.

The angel continues his explanation:

> And the ten horns which thou sawest are ten kings, which have received no kingdom as yet; but receive power as kings one hour with the beast. These have one mind, and shall give their power and strength unto the beast. These shall make war with the Lamb, and the Lamb shall overcome them: for he is Lord of lords, and King of kings: and they that are with him are called, and chosen, and faithful. (Rev. 17:12-14)

The angel has just told us about the seven heads of the beast in Revelation 17. Now he tells about the significance of the ten horns of the beast that had seven heads and ten horns. These ten horns do not have power as kings yet, because they do not yet have their crowns. When they do receive authority as kings, they will act as a united power and give their power and strength to the beast. Then the angel tells us what action we must look for. This union of powers—the ten-horned beast of Revelation 17, Babylon, and the eighth beast—will make war against the Lamb and His people (Rev. 17:14). Yet, the angel says that the Lamb will overcome them. Who is John talking about? The explanation in Daniel 2 can shed some light:

> This image's head was of fine gold, his breast and his arms of silver, his belly and his thighs of brass, his legs of iron, *his feet part of iron and part of clay*. Thou sawest till that a stone was cut out without hands, which smote the image upon his feet that were of iron and clay, and brake them to pieces. (Dan. 2:32-34, emphasis supplied)

This explanation is at the end of Daniel's description of the king's dream in Daniel 2. Having described each part of the statue in detail, Daniel tells the king that a stone from heaven will crush the metal statue and fill the earth as a mighty mountain. Then Daniel gives the king the interpretation. What Daniel says about the feet of the image is significant:

> And whereas thou sawest the feet and toes, part of potters' clay, and part of iron, the kingdom shall be divided; but there shall be in it of the strength of the iron, forasmuch as thou sawest the iron mixed with miry clay. And as *the toes of the feet* were part of iron, and part of clay, so the kingdom shall be partly strong, and partly broken …. And in the days of *these kings* shall the God of heaven set up a kingdom, which shall never be destroyed: and the kingdom shall not be left to other people, but it shall break in pieces and consume all these kingdoms, and it shall stand for ever. (Dan. 2:41, 42, 44, emphasis supplied)

Daniel says that the history of the false religion of Satan is seen in the image of Daniel 2. Each kingdom or division is represented by a different part of the image: the head, the chest, the thighs, the legs, the feet, and finally the toes. Then, Daniel declares that, in the day of the feet and toes, God will set up His kingdom. God's kingdom will not be destroyed. It will stand forever.

The ten toes of Daniel 2 are a parallel symbolic figure of the ten horns or ten kings of Revelation 17:

> And *the ten horns* which thou sawest are ten kings, which have received no kingdom as yet; but receive power as kings one hour with the beast. These [the last ten kings and Babylon] *have one mind, and shall give their power and strength unto the beast.* (Rev. 17:12, 13, emphasis supplied)

The angel is declaring that the seventh king from Revelation 13, the new world order and Babylon, will give their power and strength to the eighth beast of verse 11. "These [that is, Babylon, the last ten kings, and the eighth king] shall make war with the Lamb, and the Lamb shall overcome them: for he is Lord of lords, and King of kings: and they that are with him are called, and chosen, and faithful" (Rev. 17:14).

John gives an overview of this act of war in Revelation 12 and 13. "The dragon [through pagan Rome or spiritualism] went to make war with the remnant of her seed, which keep the commandments of God, and have the testimony of Jesus Christ" (Rev. 12:17). He also says that the composite beast (papal Rome) "was given … to make war with the saints, and to overcome them" (Rev. 13:7) and that the lamblike beast (the United States of America) "had power to give life unto the image of the beast, that the image of the beast should both speak, and cause that as many as would not worship the image of the beast should be killed" (Rev. 13:15).

The union of spiritualism, papal Rome, and apostate Protestantism constitutes *Babylon*. "These [the last ten kings and Babylon and the eighth king] shall make war with the Lamb, and the Lamb shall overcome them: for he is Lord of lords, and King of kings: and they that are with him are called, and chosen, and faithful" (Rev. 17:14).

They will make war with the Lamb, but the Lamb will overcome them because He is Lord of lords and King of kings—He is God. Then the angel tells us that those who stand with the Lamb in this warfare are "called" of God, "chosen" by God, and "faithful" to God.

> "Father, thank You for showing us the future. You have convicted us with Your Spirit. You have converted us with Your word here in Revelation. Help us to get ready to stand for You in the time of the end."

Chapter 6

God's Counter Attack

How will God respond to the power and destructiveness of Babylon and the new world order? How will He overcome His enemy when the whole world is focused on the destruction of His people? We have just studied Satan's plans in Revelation 12, 13, and 17. Now we need to study God's plans for the time of the end. How will He help His servants? What are His plans for saving mankind?

In the tenth chapter of Revelation, John "is given" a prophecy concerning the end of the world. A heavenly angel told him, "Thou must prophesy again before many peoples, and nations, and tongues, and kings" (Rev. 10:11). I believe that Jesus is talking with John and has just told him that he will prophecy again in the time of the end. If John died in the first century, how can he prophesy in the twenty-first century? Will he rise from the dead, or will the words that he wrote be carried to the ends of the earth? To ask the question is to know the answer. The prophecies of Revelation were written for our time. It is the prophecies of John's book—the revelation of Jesus Christ—that will be taken to the ends of the earth.

The vision of Revelation 11 gives God's response to the evil that will come upon this world at the time of the end. Turning to the eleventh chapter of Revelation, we read: "And there was given me a reed like unto a rod: and the angel stood, saying, Rise, and measure the temple of God, and the altar, and them that worship therein" (Rev. 11:1).

The angel's command is something that John has not been told to do before. He is asked to "measure" some things that are already standing. Let's go to Matthew and see how Jesus uses the word "measure." "Judge not, that ye be not judged. For with what judgment ye judge, ye shall be judged: and with what measure ye mete, it shall be measured to you again" (Matt. 7:1, 2).

Here, Jesus has given good counsel about judging: Do not judge according to your judgment because you will be judged by the same judgment—the same faulty, human judgment—that you use to judge others. If you must judge, judge according to God's standard. Applying this to Revelation 11:1, John is asked to measure or judge—according to God's standard—the character and meaning of the sanctuary of God, the altar of incense, and those who worship in the sanctuary. We turn to Albert Barnes for help in understanding what this means:

> *Rise, and measure the temple of God.* That is, ascertain its true dimensions with the reed in your hand. Of course, this could not be understood of the *literal* temple—whether standing or not—for the exact measure of that was sufficiently well known. The word, then, must be used of something which the temple would denote or represent …
>
> *And them that worship therein.* In the temple; or, as the temple is the representation here of the church, of those who are in the church as professed worshippers of God. There is some apparent incongruity in directing him to "*measure*" those who were engaged in worship; but the obvious meaning is, that he was to take a correct estimate of their character; of what they professed; of the reality of their piety; of their lives, and of the general state of the church considered as professedly worshipping God. (Albert Barnes, *Barnes' Notes on the New Testament* [Grand Rapids, Kregel Publications, 1980] p. 1643)

The things that John was asked to "measure" are real, and they represent important objects in God's plan for the redemption of mankind. The first of these is the temple in heaven, where God's throne resides (Rev. 4). It is also where our great High Priest intercedes for us and watches over us in God's plan of redemption and where He wants us to go in our time of need.

The altar mentioned in Revelation 11:1 is the altar of incense that was located in the holy place of the earthly sanctuary. That altar burned incense "24/7" throughout the wilderness journey of the Israelites. David defines its importance for us: "Let my prayer be set forth before thee as incense …" (Psalm 141:2). This symbolic structure located in the heavenly sanctuary is assurance that our prayers are being heard and answered by our High Priest in the heavenly sanctuary (Rev. 8:3).

The third thing John was to measure is not part of the sanctuary itself. It is the worshippers within the temple of God. Who are they? Paul describes the quality of the true believer: "I am crucified with Christ: nevertheless I live; yet not I, but Christ liveth in me: and the life which I now live in the flesh I live by the faith of the Son of God, who loved me, and gave himself for me" (Gal. 2:20). These newborn Christians look to the sanctuary in heaven for mercy and grace. They know that they can pray to their High Priest in the heavenly sanctuary for guidance. They offer themselves as messengers to carry God's message of warning and hope to the four corners of the earth. They will "sit with [Jesus] in [His] throne" (Rev. 3:21; cf. Eph. 2:6).

The angel told John that his prophecies were to go out to "many peoples, and nations, and tongues, and kings" at the time of the end (Rev. 10:11). Yet, these prophetic messages must be balanced with the knowledge of the sanctuary in heaven, the need for constant prayer, and the standard of character that each worshipper of God must have. This is the same standard that John mentioned at the beginning of the Revelation: "I … was in the isle that is called Patmos, for the word of God, and for the testimony of

Jesus Christ" (Rev. 1:9). It is the Word of God that tells us about the plan of salvation, the need of prayer, and the responsibility of the priesthood. That was the standard of character then, and it is the standard of character for those who carry the message of God to the world today. This is God's warning message: Get ready for the time of the end!

> Here is the work going on, measuring the temple and its worshipers to see who will stand in the last day. Those who stand fast shall have an abundant entrance into the kingdom of our Lord and Saviour Jesus Christ. When we are doing our work remember there is One that is watching the spirit in which we are doing it. (Ellen G. White, Ms. 4, 1888 in *The Seventh-day Adventist Bible Commentary*, vol. 7, p. 972)

> The work is going on in the heavenly court. In vision on the Isle of Patmos John said: "And there was given me a reed like unto a rod, and the angel stood, saying, Arise and measure the temple of God, and the altar, and them that worship therein." This solemn work is to be done upon the earth. Look and see how stands your measurement of character as compared with God's standard of righteousness, his holy law. The worshipers are to pass under the measuring line of God. Who will bear the test? (Ellen G. White, *The Youth's Instructor*, Aug. 25, 1886)

John's list of things to measure includes "the temple of God, and the altar, and them that worship therein." We can compare this list with the one that was given to the composite beast: "And he opened his mouth in blasphemy against God, to blaspheme his name, and his tabernacle, and them that dwell in heaven" (Rev. 13:6). This composite beast has an agenda. Yet, God has the answer in Revelation 11: Be sure of your foundation; study to show yourself approved unto God; then you may say with John, I am on this earth "for the word of God, and for the testimony of Jesus Christ." The angel gives John more instructions: "But the court which is without the temple leave out, and measure it not; for it is given unto the Gentiles: and the holy city shall they tread under foot forty and two months" (Rev. 11:2).

The angel is saying: *Measure and understand the temple of God, the altar, and those who worship at the temple, but don't measure the outer court.* In the wilderness, the sanctuary was surrounded by a rectangle of linen that was 50 by 100 cubits in length and width, and five cubits high. The area within this linen wall was called the outer court. It was the area that sinners among the Israelites could enter with their sacrifices for sin. Through the linen gate on the eastern side, they approached the altar of sacrifice, where a priest assisted them with the symbolic sacrifice of the lamb. The priest then placed the spilt blood of the sacrifice on the altar of sacrifice or, in certain cases, before the curtain in the holy place of the sanctuary. The spilt blood met the demands of the law for the sinner. In this way, the sinner exited the outer court with his sin covered by the blood of the sacrifice.

The outer court was the area that was given to the Gentiles. There are two essential facts about this outer court. First, the altar of sacrifice was located within the outer court. On this altar every sacrifice was burned to ashes. The ashes symbolized the wages of sin, for Paul tells us that "the wages of sin is death" (Rom. 6:23). But the altar of sacrifice also symbolized the gift of God for mankind. Thus, the altar was a foreshadowing of the place of sacrifice on the cross. Jesus was the Lamb offered for our sins, and the altar of burnt offering reveals the completeness of His gift. He gave His life on the cross that all our sins might be covered by His blood (Gal. 2:20). Yet, in John's vision, the outer court was *given* to the Gentiles, to those who did not worship Him. Could it be that He is still trying to win sinners over by displaying this symbol of His love?

Second, the outer court of the sanctuary of David was part of the city of Jerusalem. So, when the angel says that "the holy city shall they tread under foot forty and two months" (Rev. 11:2), we are being told that the Gentiles will not only force their political agenda on the city of Jerusalem, but they will spread their false religion within the modern church of Jesus Christ. They will trample under foot the city of Jerusalem and the religious ideals that the outer court represents. This unholy influence was to last for forty-two months, or 1,260 days. The Gentiles' treading under foot is covered in *Barnes' Notes on the New Testament*:

> *Shall they tread under foot.* That is, the Gentiles above referred to; or those who, in the measurement of the city, were set off as Gentiles, and regarded as not belonging to the people of God. This is not spoken of the Gentiles in general, but only of that portion of the multitudes that seemed to constitute the worshippers of God, who, in measuring the temple, were set off or separated as not properly belonging to the true church. The phrase "should tread under foot" is derived from warriors and conquerors who tread down their enemies, or trample on the fields of grain. It is rendered in this passage by Dr. Robinson (*Lex.*,) "to profane and lay waste." As applied literally to a city, this would be the true ideal; as applied to the church, it would mean that they would have it under their control or in subjection for the specified time, and that the practical effect of that would be to corrupt and prostrate it. (Albert Barnes, *Barnes' Notes on the New Testament* [Grand Rapids, MI: Kregel Publications, 1962], p. 1644)

In Scripture, "Gentiles" literally means "the nations" and describes anyone who worships false gods and does not follow the true God. This angel is telling us that the sacred outer court of the sanctuary will be under their control. They will profane it, lay it waste, corrupt it, and prostrate it for forty-two months.

For now, we need to return to the narrative, but we will address this evil action of the Gentiles later. "And I will give *power* unto my two witnesses, and they shall prophesy a thousand two hundred and threescore days, clothed in sackcloth" (Rev. 11:3).

Then, in verse 3, the angel tells John that God will give something to the two witnesses. He tells us that the witnesses, clothed with sackcloth, will prophecy for about 1,260 days. We know that these 1,260 days are equal to three and a half years. These three and a half years are equal to the same amount of time that was designated for the early rain. Could this time period of the two witnesses be the time of the latter rain? Let's go on. "These are the two olive trees, and the two candlesticks standing before the God of the earth" (Rev. 11:4).

What is the angel telling us? Let's go back to verse 3. The King James Version tells us that God will "give power unto my two witnesses." That word "power" is not in the Greek. It was added by translators for clarification of the context. The text should read: "I will give unto my two witnesses." The next question is obvious. What is it that God will give the two witnesses? We are not told in verse 3. The angel goes on and says that both witnesses will prophecy 1,260 days in sackcloth. Then he tells us in verse 4 what the gift is that He is giving. He says that the gifts are "two olive trees … standing before the God of the earth."

Let's go back and study some of these phrases. First, who are these two witnesses? Second, why are they dressed in sackcloth? And third, why are heavenly angels giving the two witnesses a double portion of the Holy Spirit that comes from the anointed ones in heaven?

The two witnesses are God's representatives. Jesus gave us a definition of witnesses in the Gospel of Matthew:

> Moreover if thy brother shall trespass against thee, go and tell him his fault between thee and him alone: if he shall hear thee, thou hast gained thy brother. But if he will not hear thee, then take with thee one or two more, that in the mouth of two or three witnesses every word may be established. (Matt. 18:15, 16)

Jesus tells us that if your brother will not confess to a wrong he did against you, take one or two friends with you and confront him again. In this second confrontation, you will have two or more witnesses. So that every word that you or your adversary says will be established by the witnesses. You need two witnesses to verify what was said in a conversation or a discussion or a court scene. These two witnesses in Revelation 11 have seen the same scenes. When one says: *I saw this and that*, the other will say: *I saw this and that too*. Their testimonies are verified by each other. Their testimonies can be trusted.

John, in the New Testament era, tells us that he was a witness. He is a witness of the prophecies of Jesus Christ in Revelation:

> I, John, your brother and companion—sharer and participator—with you in the tribulation and kingdom and patient endurance [which are] in Jesus *Christ,* was on the isle called Patmos, [banished] on account of [my witnessing to] the Word of God and the testimony—the proof, the evidence—for Jesus *Christ.* (Rev. 1:9, AMP).

Daniel, in the Old Testament era, was also a witness. At the end of the book of Daniel, God tells him to "go thou thy way till the end be: for thou shalt rest, and stand in thy lot at the end of the days" (Dan. 12:13). What does this idea of "standing in your lot" mean?

> Each one is to stand in his lot and in his place, doing his work. Every individual among you must before God do a work for these last days that is great and sacred and grand. Every one must bear his weight of responsibility.... (Ellen G. White, Letter 49, 1897 in *Manuscript Releases*, vol. 21, p. 336)

In other words, you have your own work to do; you have your own responsibilities. So how does this principle apply to Daniel and John?

> A wonderful connection is here seen between the universe of heaven and this world. The things revealed to Daniel were afterward complemented by the revelation made to John on the isle of Patmos. These two books should be carefully perused.... But go thou thy way till the end be: for thou shalt rest, and stand in thy lot at the end of the days" [Dan. 12:8–10, 13].
>
> It was the Lion of the tribe of Judah who unsealed the book and gave to John the revelation of what should be in these last days. Daniel stood in his lot to bear his testimony, which was sealed until the time of the end, when the first angel's message should be proclaimed to our world.... (Ellen G. White, Letter 59, 1896 in *Manuscript Releases*, vol. 18, p. 15)

In 1844 the book of Daniel was unsealed through an understanding of the book of Revelation:

> As we near the close of this world's history, the prophecies recorded by Daniel demand our special attention, as they relate to the very time in which we are living. With them should be linked the teachings of the last book of the New Testament Scriptures.... (Ellen G. White, *Prophets and Kings*, p. 547)

The prophecies of Daniel are to be studied as they relate to our time. The prophecies of Daniel are to be linked with the teachings of Revelation. Who wrote these books? Daniel and John. Who then are these two witnesses of Revelation 11? I believe it is Daniel and John. Revelation tells how the prophecies of Daniel and Revelation will be carried to the four corners of the world.

Concerning the fact that the two witnesses are wearing sackcloth, the Jamieson-Fausset-Brown Bible *Commentary* tells us that sackcloth was worn by prophets "especially when calling people to mortification of their sins, and to repentance" (Jamieson-Fausset-Brown, *A Commentary*, vol. 2, p. 574).

What was said about the time of the vision? "And I will give *power* unto my two witnesses, and they shall prophesy a thousand two hundred and threescore days, clothed in sackcloth" (Rev. 11:3). The angel tells us that these two witnesses have a special time. They will prophesy for 1,260 days (verse 3). When they have finished their testimony, the beast will make war against them and kill them (verse 7). When the two witnesses have rested for three and a half days, God will raise them up in a cloud to heaven (verse 11).

Before we examine the work of the two witnesses, we need to understand the story of the olive trees and the candlesticks found in Zechariah 4, which will help us understand Revelation 11:4:

> And the angel that talked with me came again, and waked me, as a man that is wakened out of his sleep, And said unto me, What seest thou? And I said, I have looked, and behold a candlestick all of gold, with a bowl upon the top of it, and his seven lamps thereon, and seven pipes to the seven lamps, which are upon the top thereof: And two olive trees by it, one upon the right side of the bowl, and the other upon the left side thereof. So I answered and spake to the angel that talked with me, saying, What are these, my lord? Then the angel that talked with me answered and said unto me, Knowest thou not what these be? And I said, No, my lord. Then he answered and spake unto me, saying, This is the word of the LORD unto Zerubbabel, saying, Not by might, nor by power, but by my spirit, saith the LORD of hosts. Who art thou, O great mountain? before Zerubbabel thou shalt become a plain: and he shall bring forth the headstone thereof with shoutings, crying, Grace, grace unto it ... Then answered I, and said unto him, What are these *two olive trees* upon the right side of the *candlestick* and upon the left side thereof? And I answered again, and said unto him, What be these two olive branches which through the two golden pipes empty the golden oil out of themselves? And he answered me and said, Knowest thou not what these be? And I said, No, my lord. Then said he, *These are the two anointed ones that stand by the Lord of the whole earth.* (Zech. 4:1–7, 11–14, emphasis supplied)

Zechariah was shown how the Holy Spirit is poured into the candlestick in the Most Holy Place of the temple of God. In verses 2 and 3, Zechariah tells the angel that he sees the lampstand that sits in the heavenly sanctuary. Leslie Hardinge expands on the meaning of these symbols:

> The lampstand's central pillar sent forth six branches. ... Christians are the "branches" begotten through the Spirit to be lights in the world through their holy lives (2 Pet 1:4; 1 Pet 1:23). The Spirit speaks of these six branches as though they were one, because they grew from a single source. Their unity fulfils our High Priest's prayer for His disciples (John 17:11, 21, 22). Across the centuries their gospel hymn is: "The seven candlesticks are the seven churches" (Rev 1:20).... they are united in their Saviour as boughs are in a tree.... the place of the disciple is on the candlestick (Matt 5:14), that is, in the church (Rev 1:20).... To help us to become light-bearers God has given "us exceeding great and precious promises: that by these we may be partakers of the divine nature" (2 Pet 1:3, 4). ... The candlestick is thus a symbol of the work, not only of Christ and His regenerate church, but also of each new-born disciple. Then lift the living Torch high, for this glorious task alone the lampstand was fashioned, the church

called, and we are born again. (Leslie Hardinge, *Through the Tabernacle Along His Way with Jesus in His Sanctuary* [Harrisburg, PA: American Cassette Ministries, 1991], pp. 149, 151)

Zechariah tells us that on either side of the candlestick he saw an olive tree. In verse 6, he is told that the candlestick represents the Holy Spirit. Yet, in verse 12 we notice that Zechariah did not understand what the two olive trees represented, so he asks about them. In verse 14, he is told. These are the anointed ones, or cherubs, that stand by Jesus Christ in the heavenly sanctuary. What should we understand from the text?

> The psalmist says, "Thy word is a lamp unto my feet, and a light unto my path." Psalm 119:105. The oil is a symbol of the Holy Spirit.... (Ellen G. White, *Christ's Object Lessons*, p. 406)

> ... So from the holy ones that stand in God's presence His Spirit is imparted to the human instrumentalities who are consecrated to His service. The mission of the two anointed ones is to communicate to God's people that heavenly grace which alone can make His word a lamp to the feet and a light to the path.... (*Christ's Object Lessons*, p. 408)

The oil is the symbol of the Holy Spirit. This vision is telling us that God is pouring His Spirit into His two witnesses by way of the "anointed ones" that stand next to Him. How does the author describe the effect of the Spirit?

> So from the holy ones that stand in God's presence, His Spirit is imparted to human instrumentalities that are consecrated to His service. The mission of the two anointed ones is to communicate light *and power* to God's people. It is to receive blessing for us that they stand in God's presence. As the olive trees empty themselves into the golden pipes, so the heavenly messengers seek to communicate all that they receive from God. The whole heavenly treasure awaits our demand and reception; and as we receive the blessing, we in our turn are to impart it. Thus it is that the holy lamps are fed, and the church becomes a light bearer in the world. (Ellen G. White, *Testimonies to Ministers*, p. 510, emphasis supplied)

The holy lamps are filled with the Spirit of God. In the vision of Zechariah, the one candlestick represents the work of the Holy Spirit. Yet, in Revelation 11:4, the two candlesticks seen in this vision represent a double blessing. They will fill the two witnesses with a double portion of the Spirit of God. These witnesses become the light bearers for the world at the time of the end. Their mission will be filled with truth and power from God so they can proclaim the gospel of Jesus Christ and the prophecies of

Jesus Christ to the world. What is it that God wants us to do for Him?

> This is the work that the Lord would have every soul prepared to do at this time, when the four angels are holding the four winds, that they shall not blow until the servants of God are sealed in their foreheads. There is no time now for self-pleasing. The lamps of the soul must be trimmed. They must be supplied with the oil of grace. Every precaution must be taken to prevent spiritual declension, lest the great day of the Lord overtake us as a thief in the night. Every witness for God is now to work intelligently in the lines which God has appointed. We should daily obtain a deep and living experience in the work of perfecting Christian character. We should daily receive the holy oil, that we may impart to others. All may be light bearers to the world if they will. We are to sink self out of sight in Jesus. We are to receive the word of the Lord in counsel and instruction, and gladly communicate it. There is now need of much prayer. Christ commands, "Pray without ceasing;" that is, keep the mind uplifted to God, the source of all power and efficiency. (Ellen G. White, *Testimonies to Ministers*, p. 510)

The counsel of the servant of God is clear: "We should daily receive the holy oil, that we may impart to others. All may be light bearers to the world if they will."

These two witnesses have been empowered with the gift of the Spirit of God. Because there are two candlesticks, we must assume that these two witnesses are receiving a double portion of the Spirit of God. These two witnesses are receiving the latter rain. This special gift of the latter rain will be given to the two witnesses in the "appointed time" of the end.

Let's continue our study. The next verse tells us that these two witnesses are not meek and mild: "And if any man will hurt them, fire proceedeth out of their mouth, and devoureth their enemies: and if any man will hurt them, he must in this manner be killed" (Rev. 11:5).

Can you believe those words? The New International Version puts it this way: "If anyone tries to harm them, fire comes from their mouths and devours their enemies. This is how anyone who wants to harm them must die" (Rev. 11:5). We know from James what a problem the tongue can be:

> Even so the tongue is a little member, and boasteth great things. Behold, how great a matter a little fire kindleth! And the tongue is a fire, a world of iniquity: so is the tongue among our members, that it defileth the whole body, and setteth on fire the course of nature; and it is set on fire of hell. (James 3:5, 6)

So is this principle true of the two witnesses? Are their tongues set on fire of hell? In the Psalms, David described the consuming nature of God's word: "Smoke rose from his nostrils; consuming fire came from his mouth, burning coals blazed out of it. (Psalm 18:8, NIV)

Is there a verse that describes what God wants to see in His people? Yes, there is. "Therefore this is what the Lord God Almighty says: 'Because the people have spoken these words, I will make my words in your mouth a fire and these people the wood it consumes'" (Jer. 5:14, NIV).

In this last verse, God is describing what He will do with the words of Jeremiah. Is He not describing the same effect for the words of the two witnesses? Those words may not kindle forest fires, but they will make the enemies of God think twice about harming God's two witnesses. "These have power to shut heaven, that it rain not in the days of their prophecy: and have power over waters to turn them to blood, and to smite the earth with all plagues, as often as they will" (Rev. 11:6).

What authority will be given to those who give the prophecies of the two witnesses? God's word has authority to cause the clouds to cease from raining. Does that not sound like what Elijah did? God's word has authority to turn the waters into blood: to strike the earth with plagues. Does that not sound like what Moses did?

> "The keys of the kingdom of heaven" are the words of Christ. All the words of Holy Scripture are His, and are here included. These words have power to open and to shut heaven. They declare the conditions upon which men are received or rejected. Thus the work of those who preach God's word is a savor of life unto life or of death unto death. Theirs is a mission weighted with eternal results. (Ellen G. White, *The Desire of Ages*, p. 413)

The King James Version renders verse 7: "And when they shall have finished their testimony, the beast that ascendeth out of the bottomless pit shall make war against them, and shall overcome them, and kill them" (Rev. 11:7). The Amplified version puts it this way: "But when they have finished their testimony *and* their evidence is all in, the beast (monster) that comes up out of the Abyss (bottomless pit) will wage war on them, and conquer them and kill them" (Rev. 11:7, AMP).

Let's summarize this last verse. The angel says that when the two witnesses finish their witness and have given all their evidence from the Bible, at the end of the 1,260 days, a beast will come against them. He then identifies this beast as the one that ascends from the pit. This beast will declare war against these two prophets and their witness. The angel then tells us that this beast will overcome them and then kill them.

Wow! As the witnesses of God are presenting the prophecies of Daniel and Revelation according to the will of God, with the power of the latter rain, John tells us that a beast will arise to make war against them. And not only that, but he will succeed in killing them! How can this be? Isn't God leading these two witnesses? Doesn't God win every battle?

Who is the beast that comes out of the pit? The book of Revelation contains clues to the identification of this beast. Where does this beast come from? The text says it comes from the bottomless pit. References to the bottomless pit are found in Revelation chapters 9, 17, and 20. We begin with the one in chapter 17:

> The beast that thou sawest was, and is not; and shall ascend out of the bottomless pit, and go into perdition: and they that dwell on the earth shall wonder, whose names were not written in the book of life from the foundation of the world, when they behold the beast that was, and is not, and yet is. (Rev. 17:8)

This verse tells us that there is a one beast that was seen in world events, then disappears, and then reappears on the world scene. But it also tells us that this beast, after ascending from the "bottomless pit," will be thrown into perdition. The next passage of the "pit" is in chapter 20:

> And I saw an angel come down from heaven, having the key of the bottomless pit and a great chain in his hand. And he laid hold on the dragon, that old serpent, which is the Devil, and Satan, and bound him a thousand years, and cast him into the bottomless pit, and shut him up, and set a seal upon him, that he should deceive the nations no more, till the thousand years should be fulfilled: and after that he must be loosed a little season. (Rev. 20:1–3)

John declares that, after the second coming, Satan will be cast by an angel of God into the "bottomless pit" for a thousand years. At the end of those years, he will be "loosed" for a while. If he is put into the "bottomless pit" by an angel, would it not be logical that an angel will loose him from it? The next verses describe when he will be loosed.

> And the fifth angel sounded, and I saw a star fall from heaven unto the earth: and to him was given the key of the bottomless pit. And he opened the bottomless pit; and there arose a smoke out of the pit, as the smoke of a great furnace; and the sun and the air were darkened by reason of the smoke of the pit ... And they had a king over them, which is the angel of the bottomless pit, whose name in the Hebrew tongue is Abaddon, but in the Greek tongue hath his name Apollyon. (Rev. 9:1, 2, 11)

Here John describes an action occurring on earth. A star—or angel of heaven—is given the key to the bottomless pit and opens it. Locusts like smoke arise from the bottomless pit and the king of the locusts is also released from it. The king's name is Abaddon and Apollyon—both names mean destroyer. The king that was released from the pit is the one who was put into the pit. Who is known as our destroyer?

> Satan is the great enemy of God and man. He transforms himself through his agents into angels of light. In the Scriptures he is called *a destroyer*, an accuser of the brethren, a deceiver, a liar, a tormentor, and a murderer.... (*Testimonies for the Church*, vol. 5, p. 137, emphasis supplied)

> The standard which every parent must raise is given: "They shall keep the way of the Lord." Every other way is a path which leads, not to the city of God, but to the ranks of *the destroyer*. (*Child Guidance*, p. 25, emphasis supplied)

> When any part of the body sustains injury, a healing process is at once begun; nature's agencies are set at work to restore soundness. But the power working through these agencies is the power of God. All life-giving power is from Him. When one recovers from disease, it is God who restores him. Sickness, suffering, and death are work of an antagonistic power. Satan is *the destroyer*; God is the restorer. (*Ministry of Healing*, p. 112, 113, emphasis supplied)

Satan is known as the destroyer. He is the one who tries to destroy us. He is the one who will destroy the witness of the two prophets of Revelation 11. He is the one who will "stand in the holy place" (Matt. 24:15). But God tells us that he is also the one who will eventually be shut up in the "bottomless pit," at the time of the second coming of Jesus, and released from the "bottomless pit" at the time of the third coming of Jesus Christ (Rev. 20:3). These two events have not yet been seen, but they will be seen in the near future. What is important for us to understand is that Satan is the one who will rise up against the preaching of the two witnesses. He is the one who will make war against them. He is the one who will kill these two prophets of God.

> Never did this message apply with greater force than it applies today. More and more the world is setting at nought the claims of God. Men have become bold in transgression. The wickedness of the inhabitants of the world has almost filled up the measure of their iniquity. This earth has almost reached the place where God will permit the destroyer to work his will upon it. (Ellen G. White, *Testimonies for the Church*, vol. 7, p. 141)

> Lord, help me. I am determined to cast my helpless soul upon Thee. Satan is the destroyer. Christ is the Restorer. This is Thy word to me. I will try to walk by faith. (Ellen G. White, Letter 114, 1895 in *The Australian Years 1891-1900*, p. 228)

And their dead bodies shall lie in the street of the great city, which spiritually is called Sodom and Egypt, where also our Lord was crucified (Rev. 11:8).

The bodies of the two witnesses will lie in the street of a great city: this city has been likened to the evil cities of Sodom and Egypt. Those were two places where the heathen worshipped idols. Then the angel tells us that this city is where Jesus was crucified. Doesn't that mean that this city in Revelation 11:8 is Jerusalem?

Revelation 11:2 tells us more about the city of Jerusalem. "[The outer court] is given unto the

Gentiles: and *the holy city* shall they tread under foot forty and two months" (emphasis supplied). The court of the sanctuary was located within the city limits of Jerusalem. So when the angel tells us that the court was given to the Gentiles, he was also telling us that for forty-two months, or three and a half years, the Gentiles will tread under the principles and laws of the sanctuary in Jerusalem.

The Gentiles will have control of the city of Jerusalem, thinking that they have control of the religion of the world. But this is their mistake. They will control the physical Jerusalem with military might for a time, but God's truth will ultimately rule.

This city will be used as a place of confrontation between Satan and the two witnesses, for the angel says: "And their dead bodies shall lie in the street of the great city, which spiritually is called Sodom and Egypt, where also our Lord was crucified" (Rev. 11:8). I believe Jerusalem will be the center of Babylon's worldwide work.

> And there followed another angel, saying, Babylon is fallen, is fallen, that great city, because she made all nations drink of the wine of the wrath of her fornication. (Rev. 14:8)

> And they of the people and kindreds and tongues and nations shall see their dead bodies three days and an half, and shall not suffer their dead bodies to be put in graves. And they that dwell upon the earth shall rejoice over them, and make merry, and shall send gifts one to another; because these two prophets tormented them that dwelt on the earth. (Rev. 11:9, 10)

Because the two witnesses tormented the people on earth with the prophecies of Jesus Christ from the books of Daniel and Revelation, Satan will gloat in his victory. The physical evidence that the prophets were destroyed will not be buried. In fact, Revelation says that the people of the earth will celebrate their destruction. Is this not evidence that this obscene gesture will occur right before the end of the time of the end?

All this action seems to be surrounding the great city of Jerusalem. Daniel 11:45 tells us that the king of the North "shall plant the tabernacles of his palace between the seas in the glorious holy mountain" right before the great High Priest, who stands up at the end of the time of the end.

This same theme of end-time events is seen in Matthew 24:15, 16, where Jesus describes "the abomination of desolation" standing in the Holy Place in the earthly sanctuary. "When ye therefore shall see the abomination of desolation, spoken of by Daniel the prophet, stand in the holy place …. Then let them which be in Judaea flee into the mountains." Yet, the angel does not end the vision with the destruction of the witnesses.

We read: "And after three days and an half the Spirit of life from God entered into them, and they stood upon their feet; and great fear fell upon them which saw them" (Rev. 11:11). The power of God is then witnessed. The angel says that the world will see this resurrection of the two witnesses.

That will be when they realize that the message of the witnesses was truly from God. That is when they will fear that they have chosen the wrong side. "And they heard a great voice from heaven saying unto them, Come up hither. And they ascended up to heaven in a cloud; and their enemies beheld them" (Rev. 11:12).

Jesus calls His witnesses up to heaven. They ascend in a cloud while the enemies of God look on. "And the same hour was there a great earthquake, and the tenth part of the city fell, and in the earthquake were slain of men seven thousand: and the remnant were affrighted, and gave glory to the God of heaven" (Rev. 11:13).

The angel gives us a little more information. At the time of the second coming and the ascension of the witnesses, there will be a great earthquake that will shake the earth. Yet, the righteous will give glory to God.

What will be God's answer to the power and destructiveness of Babylon and new world order? How will He succeed when the whole world is focused on the destruction of His people? The answer is found in Isaiah. "When the enemy shall come in like a flood, the Spirit of the Lord shall lift up a standard against him" (Isa. 59:19). The prophecies of Revelation were written for our time. It is the prophecies of his book that will be taken to the ends of the earth. This vision in Revelation 11 gives God's answer for the evil that will come upon this world. His answer will be seen in the character of His sons and daughters. His message of warning will go to the four corners of the earth. Then the end shall come.

> "Father, hear our prayer. Help us to be fit vessels for the outpouring of the Holy Spirit. Help us to get ready to face the enemy of the universe at the time of the end. Help us to stand for You."

Chapter 7

Prophetic Jigsaw Puzzle

We have found that Revelation, chapters 12, 13, and 17, provide details of the plans of the enemy of God for the time of the end. How do the pieces all fit together? We need to catch the big picture that God wants us to see.

When we studied Revelation 17, we found that the books of Daniel and Revelation gave us clues to understand the verse that says: "And there are seven kings: five are fallen, and one is, and the other is not yet come; and when he cometh, he must continue a short space" (Rev. 17:10). Daniel 7 lists five kingdoms. Revelation 12 and 13 list four. These kingdoms fit into two diagrams.

	Beasts from Daniel 7	
1	Lion	Babylon
2	Bear	Medo-Persia
3	Leopard	Greece
4	Dreaded Beast	Pagan Rome
5	Little Horn	Papal Rome

	Beasts from Revelation 12 and 13	
1	Red Dragon	Pagan Rome
2	Composite Beast	Papal Rome
3	Lamblike Beast	United States of America
4	Image to the Beast	Satan's New World Order

After considering these two diagrams, we realized that the fourth and fifth beasts from Daniel 7 were the same as the first and second beasts of Revelation 12 and 13. We combined the lists and renumbered them as follows:

Beasts from Daniel 7 and Revelation 12 and 13

1st	Lion	Babylon
2nd	Bear	Medo-Persia
3rd	Leopard	Greece
4th	Dreaded Beast or Red Dragon	Pagan Rome
5th	Little Horn or Composite Beast	Papal Rome
6th	Lamblike Beast	United States of America
7th	Image to the Beast	Satan's New World Order

Here are the seven kingdoms mentioned in Revelation 17, using this same numbering system as we study the big picture from Revelation 12, 13, and 17. Let's begin by looking at the struggle between the church of God and pagan Rome in chapter 12. We will place major historical events in the horizontal boxes. We will start with activity between the woman and the red dragon from Revelation 12 and place them in the vertical boxes.

Revelation 12, 13, and 17

The Woman Rev. 12:1	Woman's last days of pregnancy (12:2)	Woman delivers child, who is called to heaven (12:6)	Woman is in the wilderness for a time, times, and half a time (12:14)		Woman protected as the earth swallows the flood (12:16)	The remnant of the woman's seed (12:17)
The Red Dragon Rev. 12:3	4th beast is ready to devour the child (12:4) [1]		4th beast persecutes the woman (12:13) [2]		4th beast spews a flood out of its mouth to drown the woman (12:15) [3]	4th beast makes war with the remnant (12:17) [4]

This chronological diagram of Revelation 12 lists the various conflicts between the church of God and the dragon under its various guises, from the time of Christ to the time of the end. It begins with the great red dragon trying to destroy the Christ child [1]. In the middle of the diagram, the red dragon persecutes the church of Christ during the Middle Ages [2]. To the far right, the red dragon makes war against the woman's seed at the time of the end [4]. Backing up, just before the time of the end, the red dragon sends out a flood to drown the woman [3], yet God protects the woman by having the earth swallow the flood.

This graph is important for us to understand. It is a visual diagram of the historical events of the church of God versus one of the enemies of God: pagan Rome. This graph illustrate important events from the time of Christ to the time of the end. We see the dragon attacking God's church, but God protects them. He attacks them again, and again God protects them. Then we see the dragon taking the final step. He wages war against the church of God, but God reacts in a different way. In the time of the end, God lifts up His standard—the character of His church begins to shine. How will they be able to stand against this dragon? What will be their message to the world?

God does not end His vision to John in chapter 12. Revelation 13 describes three other enemies of God's church, whose activities parallel the activities of the church of God. God has provided these details of what His enemies are planning to do to give you the big picture of what is to come. God wants you to recognize that when the events foretold begin to take place around you that your redemption is near. The end of sin is coming, but a major battle will occur right before the end. God wants you to get ready and warn others.

The next diagram adds the parallel history of the composite beast in Revelation 13.

Revelation 12, 13, and 17

The Woman Rev. 12:1	Woman's last days of pregnancy (12:2)	Woman delivers child, who is called to heaven (12:6)	Woman is in the wilderness for a time, times, and half a time (12:14)		Woman protected as the earth swallows the flood (12:16)	The remnant of the woman's seed (12:17)	
The Red Dragon Rev. 12:3	4th beast is ready to devour the child (12:4)		4th beast persecutes the woman (12:13)		4th beast spews a flood out of its mouth to drown the woman (12:15)	4th beast makes war with the remnant (12:17)	
The Composite Beast Rev. 13:1	4th beast gives 5th beast his power, seat, and authority (13:2)	5th beast receives mortal wound to head (13:3)	5th beast's wound is healed (13:3). The world worships the dragon, which gave power to the beast and the composite beast (13:4)		5th beast is given a mouth to blaspheme God's name, God's temple, God's people for 42 months (13:5–6)	5th beast makes war with the saints (13:7)	* Given power over the world (13:8) *The world worships the beast
	[1]	[2]	[3]	[4]	[5]	[6]	[7]

We have seen in Revelation that the activities of the composite beast will parallel some of the events concerning the woman and the red dragon. The composite beast is given power from the red dragon [1]. That is to say, pagan Rome gave papal Rome its power, seat, and authority. John tells us that the next major event is the mortal wound of the head. We know from history that this event occurred in 1798 [2].

The next events in the middle of the timeline of the composite beast are the healing of the mortal wound by the red dragon [3] and the world worshipping the dragon and the composite beast [4].

Besides calling for the world to worship the composite beast, for forty-two months the beast speaks against God and His name, against His temple and His people [5]. At the end of the forty-two months, the composite beast will make war against the saints of God [6].

A beast will be given power over the earth and the world will worship this beast [7]. I believe the beast being described is Satan.

The next beast we will add to the diagram is the lamblike beast of Revelation 13.

Revelation 12, 13, and 17

The Woman Rev. 12:1	Woman's last days of pregnancy (12:2)	Woman delivers child, who is called to heaven (12:6)	Woman is in the wilderness for a time, times, and half a time (12:14)		Woman protected as the earth swallows the flood (12:16)	The remnant of the woman's seed (12:17)	
The Red Dragon Rev. 12:3	4th beast is ready to devour the child (12:4)		4th beast persecutes the woman (12:13)		4th beast spews a flood out of its mouth to drown the woman (12:15)	4th beast makes war with the remnant (12:17)	
The Composite Beast Rev. 13:1		4th beast gives 5th beast his power, seat, and authority (13:2)	5th beast receives mortal wound to head (13:3)	5th beast's wound is healed (13:3). The world worships the dragon, which gave power to the beast and the composite beast (13:4)	5th beast is given a mouth to blaspheme God's name, God's temple, God's people for 42 months (13:5–6)	5th beast makes war with the saints (13:7)	* Given power over the world (13:8) *The world worships the beast
The Lamblike Beast Rev. 13:11				6th beast commands all the world to worship the composite beast (13:12) [1]	6th beast deceives the people of Earth by miracles and fire (13:13, 14) and commands the Earth to make an image to the beast (13:14, 15) [2]	6th beast gives life to the image of the beast [3]	

The lamblike beast compels all the inhabitants of earth to worship the composite beast [1]. In other words, the United States of America will act out of character. It will force the world and its inhabitants to worship papal Rome. But how could the United States of America do this? Maybe the United States will declare that its citizens must worship God on Sunday.

Next we see the miracle that tops them all. The people of earth will be deceived by the power of Satan when he performs miracles and commands fire to come down out of heaven [2]. Soon after these miracles, this beast commands the people of the earth to make an image to the first beast. The image will look like the composite beast, having seven heads and ten horns, but it will not have the crowns for the ten horns.

Then another miracle of power will be demonstrated. This beast, the power that is behind the lamblike beast, will enable another "beast," or the image of the beast, to be empowered with civil police and authority [3]. We turn next to this last "beast" of Revelation 13.

Prophetic Jigsaw Puzzle

Revelation 12, 13, and 17

The Woman Rev. 12:1	Woman's last days of pregnancy (12:2)	Woman delivers child, who is called to heaven (12:6)	Woman is in the wilderness for a time, times, and half a time (12:14)		Woman protected as the earth swallows the flood (12:16)	The remnant of the woman's seed (12:17)	
The Red Dragon Rev. 12:3	4th beast is ready to devour the child (12:4)		4th beast persecutes the woman (12:13)		4th beast spews a flood out of its mouth to drown the woman (12:15)	4th beast makes war with the remnant (12:17)	
The Composite Beast Rev. 13:1		4th beast gives 5th beast his power, seat, and authority (13:2)	5th beast receives mortal wound to head (13:3)	5th beast's wound is healed (13:3). The world worships the dragon, which gave power to the beast and the composite beast (13:4)	5th beast is given a mouth to blaspheme God's name, God's temple, God's people for 42 months (13:5–6)	5th beast makes war with the saints (13:7)	* Given power over the world (13:8) *The world worships the beast
The Lamblike Beast Rev. 13:11			6th beast commands all the world to worship the composite beast (13:12)	6th beast deceives the people of Earth by miracles and fire (13:13, 14) and commands the Earth to make an image to the beast (13:14, 15)		6th beast gives life to the image of the beast	
The "Image of the Beast" Rev. 13:14						7th beast requires all to wear the mark of the beast or die (13:13–17) [1]	

The image to the beast is the last power on earth before the appearance of the eighth beast, or Satan. This beast will act and speak like the previous beasts. It will require that all the earth and all its people to take on the mark of the beast or be destroyed [1].

This diagram condenses and organizes key information about end-time events. The composite beast will blaspheme God and His people for forty-two months. Because this activity seems to parallel the time of the red dragon "beast," I believe that this time period will be when the flood to drown the people of God will be seen. But this is not all that will be happening at that time. The lamblike beast is active. Either this power or another will be performing miracles that will deceive the world. Then the climax occurs. Satan will bring fire down from heaven, and then he will kill the two messengers from God.

Battling the Dragons

Let's use the diagram above and ask some important questions. Who are these beasts and who do they represent? Let's begin with the composite beast.

Revelation 12, 13, and 17

The Woman Rev. 12:1	Woman's last days of pregnancy (12:2)	Woman delivers child, who is called to heaven (12:6)	Woman is in the wilderness for a time, times, and half a time (12:14)		Woman protected as the earth swallows the flood (12:16)	The remnant of the woman's seed (12:17)	
The Red Dragon Rev. 12:3	4th beast is ready to devour the child (12:4)		4th beast persecutes the woman (12:13)		4th beast spews a flood out of its mouth to drown the woman (12:15)	4th beast makes war with the remnant (12:17)	
The Composite Beast Rev. 13:1	4th beast ... and au... (13:2)	5th beast ... (13:3)	5th beast's ... healed (...). The world worships the dragon, which gave power to the beast and the composite beast (13:4)	5th beast is given a mouth to blaspheme God's name, God's temple, God's people for 42 months (13:5–6)	5th beast makes war with the saints (13:7)	* Given power over the world (13:8) *The world worships the beast	
The Lamblike Beast Rev. 13:11			6th beast commands all the world to worship the composite beast (13:12)	6th beast deceives the people of Earth by miracles and fire (13:13, 14) and commands the Earth to make an image to the beast (13:14, 15)	6th beast gives life to the image of the beast		
The "Image of the Beast" Rev. 13:14					7th beast requires all to wear the mark of the beast or die (13:13–17) [1]		

Who is the composite beast?

Revelation 12, 13, and 17

The Woman Rev. 12:1	Woman's last days of pregnancy (12:2)	Woman delivers child, who is called to heaven (12:6)	Woman is in the wilderness for a time, times, and half a time (12:14)		Woman protected as the earth swallows the flood (12:16)	The remnant of the woman's seed (12:17)	
The Red Dragon Rev. 12:3	4th beast is ready to devour the child (12:4)		4th beast persecutes the woman (12:13)		4th beast spews a flood out of its mouth to drown the woman (12:15)	4th beast makes war with the remnant (12:17)	
The Composite Beast Rev. 13:1	4th beast ... and au... (13:2)	5th beast ... (13:5)	5th beast's ... healed ...). The world worships the dragon, which gave power to the beast and the composite beast (13:4)	5th beast is given a mouth to blaspheme God's name, God's temple, God's people for 42 months (13:5–6)	5th beast makes war with the saints (13:7)	* Given power over the world (13:8) *The world worships the beast	
The Lamblike Beast Rev. 13:11			6th beast commands all the world to worship the composite beast (13:12)	6th beast deceives the people of Earth by miracles and fire (13:13, 14) and commands the Earth to make an image to the beast (13:14, 15)	6th beast gives life to the image of the beast		
The "Image of the Beast" Rev. 13:14						7th beast requires all to wear the mark of the beast or die (13:13–17) [1]	

Catholicism →

We believe the composite beast is Catholicism. Next, who is the lamblike beast?

Revelation 12, 13, and 17

The Woman Rev. 12:1	Woman's last days of pregnancy (12:2)	Woman delivers child, who is called to heaven (12:6)	Woman is in the wilderness for a time, times, and half a time (12:14)		Woman protected as the earth swallows the flood (12:16)	The remnant of the woman's seed (12:17)	
The Red Dragon Rev. 12:3	4th beast is ready to devour the child (12:4)		4th beast persecutes the woman (12:13)		4th beast spews a flood out of its mouth to drown the woman (12:15)	4th beast makes war with the remnant (12:17)	
The Composite Beast Rev. 13:1	4th be— ← Catholicism and au— (13:2)		5th beast (13:3)	5th beast's healed). The world worships the dragon, which gave power to the beast and the composite beast (13:4)	5th beast is given a mouth to blaspheme God's name, God's temple, God's people for 42 months (13:5–6)	5th beast makes war with the saints (13:7)	* Given power over the world (13:8) *The world worships the beast
The Lamblike Beast Rev. 13:11		← Who is this Beast?		to worship the composite beast (13:12)	6th beast deceives the people of Earth by miracles and fire (13:13, 14) and commands the Earth to make an image to the beast (13:14, 15)	6th beast gives life to the image of the beast	
The "Image of the Beast" Rev. 13:14						7th beast requires all to wear the mark of the beast or die (13:13–17) [1]	

We believe that this lamblike beast is the United Sates of America or apostate Protestantism.

Revelation 12, 13, and 17

The Woman Rev. 12:1	Woman's last days of pregnancy (12:2)	Woman delivers child, who is called to heaven (12:6)	Woman is in the wilderness for a time, times, and half a time (12:14)		Woman protected as the earth swallows the flood (12:16)	The remnant of the woman's seed (12:17)	
The Red Dragon Rev. 12:3	4th beast is ready to devour the child (12:4)		4th beast persecutes the woman (12:13)		4th beast spews a flood out of its mouth to drown the woman (12:15)	4th beast makes war with the remnant (12:17)	
The Composite Beast Rev. 13:1	4th beast ⬅ Catholicism and authority (13:2)	5th beast (13:3)	5th beast's wound healed. The world worships the dragon, which gave power to the beast and the composite beast (13:4)	5th beast is given a mouth to blaspheme God's name, God's temple, God's people for 42 months (13:5–6)	5th beast makes war with the saints (13:7)	* Given power over the world (13:8) *The world worships the beast
The Lamblike Beast Rev. 13:11	⬅ Apostate Protestantism		to worship the composite beast (13:12)	6th beast deceives the people of Earth by miracles and fire (13:13, 14) and commands the Earth to make an image to the beast (13:14, 15)	6th beast gives life to the image of the beast	
The "Image of the Beast" Rev. 13:14						7th beast requires all to wear the mark of the beast or die (13:13–17) [1]	

Who is the red dragon?

Revelation 12, 13, and 17

The Woman Rev. 12:1	Woman's last days of pregnancy (12:2)	Woman delivers child, who is called to heaven (12:6)	Woman is in the wilderness for a time, times, and half a time (12:14)		Woman protected as the earth swallows the flood (12:16)	The remnant of the woman's seed (12:17)	
The Red Dragon Rev. 12:3	4th beast is ready [Who is this Beast?] the ch...		4th beast persecutes...		4th beast spews a flood out of its mouth to drown the woman (12:15)	4th beast makes war with the remnant (12:17)	
The Composite Beast Rev. 13:1	4th be... [Catholicism] and au... (13:2)		5th beast ... (13:3)	5th beast's ... healed ...). The world worships the dragon, which gave power to the beast and the composite beast (13:4)	5th beast is given a mouth to blaspheme God's name, God's temple, God's people for 42 months (13:5–6)	5th beast makes war with the saints (13:7)	* Given power over the world (13:8) *The world worships the beast
The Lamblike Beast Rev. 13:11		[Apostate Protestantism]		to worship the composite beast (13:12)	6th beast deceives the people of Earth by miracles and fire (13:13, 14) and commands the Earth to make an image to the beast (13:14, 15)	6th beast gives life to the image of the beast	
The "Image of the Beast" Rev. 13:14						7th beast requires all to wear the mark of the beast or die (13:13–17) [1]	

We believe that this beast, the red dragon, is papal Rome or spiritualism.

Revelation 12, 13, and 17

The Woman Rev. 12:1	Woman's last days of pregnancy (12:2)	Woman delivers child, who is called to heaven (12:6)	Woman is in the wilderness for a time, times, and half a time (12:14)		Woman protected as the earth swallows the flood (12:16)	The remnant of the woman's seed (12:17)	
The Red Dragon Rev. 12:3	4th beast is ready ← *Spiritualism* ← the c...		4th beast persecutes...		4th beast spews a flood out of its mouth to drown the woman (12:15)	4th beast makes war with the remnant (12:17)	
The Composite Beast Rev. 13:1	4th be... ← *Catholicism* ← and au... (13:2)		5th beast ... (13:3)	5th beast's ... healed ...). The world worships the dragon, which gave power to the beast and the composite beast (13:4)	5th beast is given a mouth to blaspheme God's name, God's temple, God's people for 42 months (13:5–6)	5th beast makes war with the saints (13:7)	* Given power over the world (13:8) *The world worships the beast
The Lamblike Beast Rev. 13:11	← *Apostate Protestantism* ←			to worship the composite beast (13:12)	6th beast deceives the people of Earth by miracles and fire (13:13, 14) and commands the Earth to make an image to the beast (13:14, 15)	6th beast gives life to the image of the beast	
The "Image of the Beast" Rev. 13:14						7th beast requires all to wear the mark of the beast or die (13:13–17) [1]	

These three kingdoms represent the three parts of a world religious system. Describing this union, Ellen White wrote:

> Through the two great errors, the immortality of the soul and Sunday sacredness, Satan will bring the people under his deceptions. While the former lays the foundation of spiritualism, the latter creates a bond of sympathy with Rome. The Protestants of the United States will be foremost in stretching their hands across the gulf to grasp the hand of spiritualism; they will reach over the abyss to clasp hands with the Roman power; and under the influence of this threefold union, this country will follow in the steps of Rome in trampling on the rights of conscience. (*The Great Controversy*, p. 588)

The author tells us that Satan will bring people of the earth under his deceptions through the use of two great errors. She also says that "the Protestants of the United States" will unite with "spiritualism" and with "the Roman power." This triple union will trample on the rights of conscience in the United States of America and then throughout the rest of the world.

In another place, Ellen White states that the Protestant churches and the papal power will persecute the "commandment-keeping people of God."

> Satan will work the miracles to deceive those who dwell upon the earth. Spiritualism will do its work by causing the dead to be personated. Those religious bodies who refuse to hear God's messages of warning will be under strong deception, and will unite with the civil power to persecute the saints. The Protestant churches will unite with the papal power in persecuting the commandment-keeping people of God. This is that power which constitutes the great system of persecution which will exercise spiritual tyranny over the consciences of men. (*Manuscript Releases*, vol. 14, p. 161)

Directed by the spirit of the dragon, Protestant churches will unite with papal Rome as the great system of persecution in the time of the end. Ellen White describes this draconic spirit:

> Though professing to be followers of the Lamb of God, men become imbued with the spirit of the dragon. They profess to be meek and humble but they speak and legislate with the spirit of Satan, showing by their actions that they are the opposite of what they profess to be. *This lamblike power unites with the dragon in making war upon those who keep the commandments of God and have the testimony of Jesus Christ*. And Satan unites with Protestants and papists, acting in consort with them as the god of this world, dictating to men as if they were the subjects of his kingdom, to be handled and governed and controlled as he pleases. (*Manuscript Releases*, vol. 14, p. 162, emphasis supplied)

This lamblike power will unite with the dragon in "in making war upon those who keep the commandments of God and have the testimony of Jesus Christ."

One quotation tells us that "the Protestants of the United States of America" will unite with "spiritualism" and with "the Roman power" to make a threefold union and that this union will trample the rights of conscience. The next paragraph tells us that these same powers will unite to persecute the commandment-keeping people of God, making "war upon those who keep the commandments of God and have the testimony of Jesus Christ." We can highlight this threefold union in our diagram.

Prophetic Jigsaw Puzzle

Revelation 12, 13, and 17

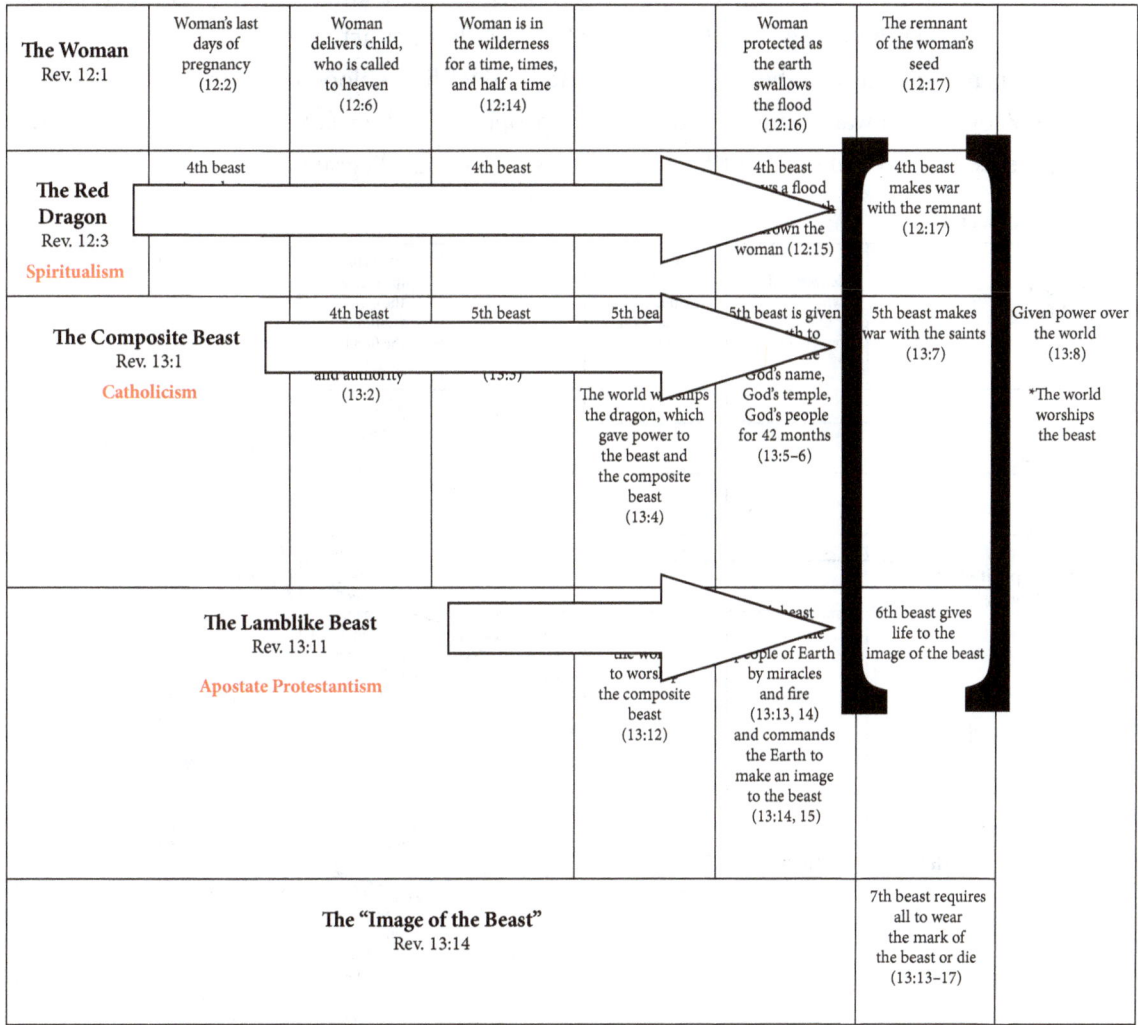

The arrows of spiritualism, Catholicism, and apostate Protestantism meet in their efforts to destroy those who keep the commandments of God and have the testimony of Jesus Christ. This is a picture of the threefold union that will trample the rights of conscience and make war against the people of God. This union rides on the seventh "beast" in Revelation 17, which has seven heads and ten horns but no crowns yet:

> So he carried me away in the spirit into the wilderness: and I saw a woman sit upon a scarlet coloured beast, full of names of blasphemy, having seven heads and ten horns. And the woman was arrayed in purple and scarlet colour, and decked with gold and precious stones and pearls, having a golden cup in her hand full of abominations and filthiness of her fornication: And upon her forehead *was* a name written, MYSTERY, BABYLON THE GREAT, THE MOTHER OF HARLOTS AND ABOMINATIONS OF THE EARTH. (Rev. 17:3–5)

From this passage, we can derive that the name of this threefold union is "Babylon." It is Babylon that will ride the seventh beast of Revelation 13. John describes her activities in the next verse. "And I saw the woman drunken with the blood of the saints, and with the blood of the martyrs of Jesus …" (Rev. 17:6). Babylon will war against and destroy the people of God for faithfully keeping all of God's commandments. We can add the identification of "Babylon" to our diagram.

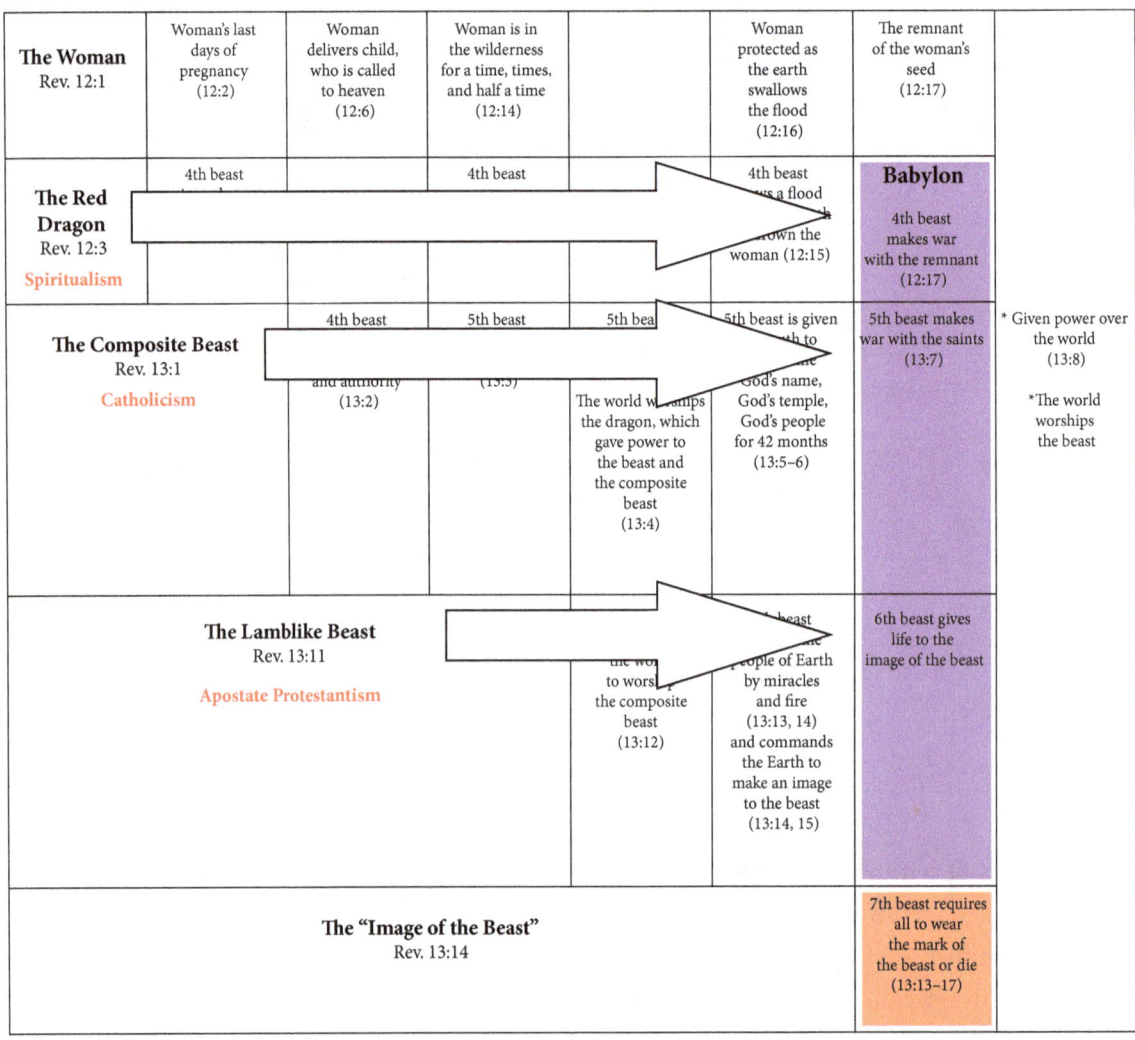

Revelation 12, 13, and 17

This explains why God gave us so much information about the beasts in Revelation 12 and 13. They each have a part to play in the time of the end. Spiritualism is based on the immortality of the soul. Believing she had the right to do so, Catholicism substituted Sunday for God's holy Sabbath. Apostate Protestantism will, like a false prophet, lead the people in accepting both of these errors. But the picture is not complete. What does John tell us about the eighth king in Revelation 17? "And there are seven kings: five are fallen, and one is, and the other is not yet come; and when he cometh, he must continue a short space. And the beast that was, and is not, even he is the eighth, and is of the seven, and goeth into perdition" (Rev. 17:10, 11).

We learned previously that Satan has made an idol for the world to worship. He started with (1) Babylon, then (2) Medo-Persia, then (3) Greece, then (4) pagan Rome, then (5) papal Rome, then (6) the United States of America, then finally (7) the new world order.

In our previous study we read that, of the seven kings, "five are fallen." That means that (1) Babylon, (2) Medo-Persia, (3) Greece, (4) pagan Rome, and (5) papal Rome have fallen from power in the world. John then tells us that "one is" and "the other is not yet come." In my estimation, this means that (6) the United States of America is the power of the world today, and (7) the new world order "will continue a short space." The eighth beast will be one that we did not see though it was nevertheless in existence. Who is this eighth beast, and where can we find him? We will highlight his presence in our diagram.

Revelation 12, 13, and 17

The Woman Rev. 12:1	Woman's last days of pregnancy (12:2)	Woman delivers child, who is called to heaven (12:6)	Woman is in the wilderness for a time, times, and half a time (12:14)		Woman protected as the earth swallows the flood (12:16)	The remnant of the woman's seed (12:17)	
The Red Dragon Rev. 12:3 Spiritualism	4th beast is ready to devour the child (12:4)	4th beast is Pagan Rom and the Devil or Satan	4th beast persecutes the woman (12:13)		4th beast spews a flood out of its mouth to drown the woman (12:15)	**Babylon** 4th beast makes war with the remnant (12:17)	
The Composite Beast Rev. 13:1 Catholicism		4th beast gives 5th beast his power, seat, and authority (13:2)	5th beast receives mortal wound to head (13:3)	5th beast's wound is healed (13:3). The world worships the dragon, which gave power to the beast and the composite beast (13:4)	5th beast is given a mouth to blaspheme God's name, God's temple, God's people for 42 months (13:5–6)	5th beast makes war with the saints (13:7)	* Given power over the world (13:8) *The world worships the beast
The Lamblike Beast Rev. 13:11 Apostate Protestantism				6th beast commands all the world to worship the composite beast (13:12)	6th beast deceives the people of Earth by miracles and fire (13:13, 14) and commands the Earth to make an image to the beast (13:14, 15)	6th beast gives life to the image of the beast	
The "Image of the Beast" Rev. 13:14						7th beast requires all to wear the mark of the beast or die (13:13–17)	

We read in the description of the red dragon in the diagram above that he is called pagan Rome and the devil or Satan. The world will worship him, together with the composite beast, when the dragon gives power to the beast once again. Through the lamblike beast, he deceives the earth with miracles and fire. In the end, he is the one who is given power over the world as all the world worships the beast that stands in the holy place of the earthly sanctuary.

This eighth beast constitutes the last column in our diagram.

Revelation 12, 13, and 17

The Woman Rev. 12:1	Woman's last days of pregnancy (12:2)	Woman delivers child, who is called to heaven (12:6)	Woman is in the wilderness for a time, times, and half a time (12:14)		Woman protected as the earth swallows the flood (12:16)	The remnant of the woman's seed (12:17)	**The Eighth Beast** *Given power over the world (13:8) *The world worships the beast
The Red Dragon Rev. 12:3 Spiritualism	4th beast is ready to devour the child (12:4)	4th beast is Pagan Rom and the Devil or Satan	4th beast persecutes the woman (12:13)		4th beast spews a flood out of its mouth to drown the woman (12:15)	**Babylon** 4th beast makes war with the remnant (12:17)	
The Composite Beast Rev. 13:1 Catholicism	4th beast gives 5th beast his power, seat, and authority (13:2)	5th beast receives mortal wound to head (13:3)	5th beast's wound is healed (13:3). The world worships the dragon, which gave power to the beast and the composite beast (13:4)	5th beast is given a mouth to blaspheme God's name, God's temple, God's people for 42 months (13:5–6)	5th beast makes war with the saints (13:7)		
The Lamblike Beast Rev. 13:11 Apostate Protestantism			6th beast commands all the world to worship the composite beast (13:12)	6th beast deceives the people of Earth by miracles and fire (13:13, 14) and commands the Earth to make an image to the beast (13:14, 15)	6th beast gives life to the image of the beast		
The "Image of the Beast" Rev. 13:14						7th beast requires all to wear the mark of the beast or die (13:13–17)	

I believe the evidence points to the eighth beast being "that old serpent, called the Devil, and Satan, which deceiveth the whole world" (Rev. 12:9). John tells us that there will be a time at the end when this eighth beast will be given power over the world. God states that this is "the beast that was, and is not, even he is the eighth, and is of the seven, and goeth into perdition" (Rev. 17:11).

When will these last-day events in this big picture begin? In our next chapter, we will look at the timeline for the end of time.

"Father, thank You for showing us what is to come. Thank You for showing us the secrets of the master plan of the enemy. Help us to understand Your plan. Help us to uncover the mask of this enemy of man. Amen."

Chapter 8
Last-Day Timelines

Mark introduces the ministry of Jesus with a statement about time: "Now after that John was put in prison, Jesus came into Galilee, preaching the gospel of the kingdom of God. And saying, The time is fulfilled, and the kingdom of God is at hand: repent ye, and believe the gospel" (Mark 1:14, 15).

The Gospel writer tells us that Jesus began His ministry preaching the good news of the kingdom of God to the people of Galilee with the prophetic statement, "The time is fulfilled." I believe that He is saying that His presence fulfilled the prophecies of the Old Testament and especially of Daniel 9:24. Following these words, Jesus tells the people that they should repent and believe the good news of God. His words imply that the good news includes prophecy, repentance, and the Word of God.

What did He mean by saying that "the kingdom of God is at hand?" God is in control of heaven and He has regained control of the Earth. He is asking each one of us, "Who has your heart? If God is not your Master, then repent and turn toward Him. Read His word. Learn of His gospel. Examine your condition. Get your family ready for the judgment to come, for the kingdom of God is near." In other words, Jesus was warning the people of Galilee that the prophetic time for the Messiah, the seventieth week of Daniel 9:24, had arrived and that they should seek repentance before God.

Let's spend a little time exploring this prophetic time in Daniel 9. Daniel was concerned about the future of Israel. He knew that Israel had been punished by God because they had fallen into idol worship rather than worshipping the true God. God had allowed the armies of Babylon to attack Jerusalem, burn the temple of God, and carry the Israelites into captivity in Babylon.

Daniel tells us that he was praying about Israel when Gabriel, the angel who stands next to God, approached him and told him that God had a message for him. Gabriel told Daniel that seventy weeks were set apart for the Messiah to establish the plan of redemption (Dan. 9:24). He told him that, from the command to restore and build Jerusalem until the Messiah would be sixty-nine prophetic weeks (Dan. 9:25). He also told him that, after the sixty-ninth week, the Messiah would confirm the covenant for one week, and that, in the middle of that seventieth week, the Messiah would die as a sacrifice for others (Dan. 9:26, 27).

Seventy weeks is equal to seventy times seven, which is equal to 490 days. I believe that Gabriel was referring to Day of Atonement days. The Day of Atonement was celebrated only one day per year, so 490 Days of Atonement equals 490 years. So how do we apply this information to the vision of Daniel 9? A comparison of Luke 3:1 with history tells us that Jesus began His ministry in the fall of AD 27. By the Passovers listed in the Gospels, we can calculate that His crucifixion outside the city walls took place on the fourth Passover after AD 27, which would have occurred in AD 31. His ministry lasted three and one half years or 42 months. According to the book of Acts, Stephen was stoned outside of Jerusalem approximately three and a half years later. This seven-year period neatly corresponds to the seventieth week of the seventy-week prophecy of Daniel 9:24.

Jesus' ministry from AD 27 to 31 is revealed in the books of Matthew, Mark, Luke, and John. It culminated with His crucifixion on the cross in AD 31. After His ascension, Jesus gave His church a special gift. He sent them the tongues of fire of the Holy Spirit, which constitutes the former rain. Because of the former rain, there was a harvest of many souls who were baptized into the church of "the Way." This former rain is the focus of the second half of the seventieth week of Daniel 9. I believe that this special gift of Jesus ended with the death of Stephen.

The next point is critical to our understanding of Revelation. We need to see and understand that the young church of Christ was empowered by the former rain for three and a half years, or forty-two months, or 1,260 days. This point will be better understood in the next few paragraphs as we consider the latter rain, because I believe that the latter rain will also last three and a half years.

God's prophetic warning is repeated in the last chapter of Revelation. An angel standing next to the throne of God declares, "Do not seal up the words of the prophecy of this book *and* make no secret of them; for the time when things are brought to a crisis *and* the period of their fulfillment is near" (Rev. 22:10, AMP). The time of crisis is upon us. We need to get ready. This verse provides the theme of the book of Revelation, which contains information about the second and the third coming of Jesus to the earth.

Just as the people of Galilee when Jesus walked on this earth were warned by a message from God, so are we at this time being warned of coming judgment from God. The fulfillment of the time prophecies of Revelation are drawing near. Jesus wants you to know that the kingdom of God is at hand. He wants you to believe the gospel of Jesus Christ, repent, and turn back to Him so that He can save you amply, fully, and entirely. Get ready and get your family and neighbors ready, for the kingdom of God is at hand.

We have concluded from studying Revelation 12, 13, and 17 that the last beast (the eighth beast) of Revelation 17 is Satan. We have also concluded that the last religious power is Babylon and that she is made up of pagan Rome (spiritualism), papal Rome (Catholicism), and the United States of America (apostate Protestantism). What we want to look at now are the references to time that are mentioned in Revelation 12 and 13 to see what they say about the beast and his image. The first timeline is in Revelation 12:

> And when the dragon saw that he was cast unto the earth, he persecuted the woman which brought forth the man child. And to the woman were given two wings of a great eagle, that she might fly into the wilderness, into her place, where she is nourished for a time, and times, and half a time, from the face of the serpent. (Rev. 12:13, 14)

John tells us in this verse that "when the dragon saw that he was cast unto the earth [after Jesus Christ had returned to heaven], he persecuted the woman which brought forth the man child" (Rev. 12:13). Then John adds: "To the woman were given two wings of a great eagle, that she might fly into the wilderness, into her place, where she is nourished for a time, and times, and half a time" (Rev. 12:14). The church of Christ was forced to flee to the wilderness because of the persecution by the dragon beast for "a time, times, and half a time." From Daniel 4, we learn that "time" is equal to one year. So this "time, times, and half a time" equals three and a half years. We studied this timeline previously and concluded that this timeline of "a time, times, and half a time," or three and a half years, which equal forty-two months or 1,260 days, is actually 1,260 Days of Atonement. Since the Day of Atonement was celebrated only one day per year, this means that these 1,260 Days of Atonement equal 1,260 years. Let's use an example to help explain how this time period, described in days, should be understood as years. Let's say that a friend is having a birthday party. This is the fiftieth time that he has celebrated his birthday. So how old is your friend? Because he has celebrated fifty birthDAYS, we know that he is now fifty years old.

The church of Christ was persecuted for "a time, times, and half a time" (Rev. 12:14). We now know that this time period is equal to 1,260 years. We believe that these 1,260 years ran from AD 538 to 1798. This is the timeline during which the dragon persecuted the church (Rev. 12:14).

This is also a timeline for the composite beast (Dan. 7:25; Rev. 13:1). From history we know that the composite beast also persecuted the church of Christ from AD 538 to 1798. Yet, in 1798 the beast received a mortal wound and was removed from earthly power for a time. Nonetheless, as we continue reading about the composite beast in the first eight verses of Revelation 13, we find that its mortal wound was to be healed and the dragon was to give it power and authority for a second time. Of this composite beast John says: "… there was given unto him a mouth speaking great things and blasphemies; and power was given unto him to continue forty and two months" (Rev. 13:5). This is the second timeline in these two chapters.

Is this period of "forty and two months" (Rev. 13:5) equal to 1,260 days, or is it equal to 1,260 years, as in the time period of Revelation 12:14? The use of the word "months" (Rev. 13:5) gives us the clue we need. In Revelation 12:14 we are told that the church would be protected for three and a half years. We know from history that the church was protected for 1,260 years of persecution from the composite beast.

But in Revelation 13:5 this same composite beast is given forty-two months to persecute the church again after its wound had been healed. If the wound was healed in 1798, are we to look for this next persecution in 1,260 years? I don't think so. It is my belief that this "forty-two months" is the same "forty-two months" from Revelation 11:2, because the character of the composite beast in Revelation 13 is the same character of the Gentiles in Revelation 11. These "forty-two months" of Revelation 13:5 are actually forty-two consecutive months.

What activities will the composite beast engage in during these forty-two months? John tells us that "… he opened his mouth in blasphemy against God, to blaspheme his name, and his tabernacle, and them that dwell in heaven" (Rev. 13:6).

John sees the composite beast blaspheming the name of God, the temple of God, and the people that worship God after it has received power and authority from the dragon beast for the second time. Then John tells us that "it was given unto him to make war with the saints, and to overcome them" (Rev. 13:7). It is to "him" that the right to declare war with the saints will be given that they might be overcome and destroyed. But we must ask a question. Who is the "him" in the passage? Who is this beast that will make war with the saints? Is it the composite beast that was given life again by the dragon? Or is it the dragon beast that gave life to the composite beast? Let's assume that the "him" is the composite beast. What kind of political power does this composite beast have if he has to be *given* the right to make war with the saints (Rev. 13:7)? That phrase implies that the composite beast does not have the power of the dragon beast. Doesn't the greater always have glory above the lesser? Doesn't this mean that it is the composite beast that is told what to do?

This second chance at world power for the composite beast comes after this beast has its mortal wound healed by the dragon beast. Since we have not seen the dragon beast at the center stage of world power, nor seen his ability to resurrect the composite beast, I believe that this event has not yet occurred. However, God has given us signs to look for. Returning to the text, we find that the composite beast was given "a mouth speaking great things and blasphemies; and power was given unto him to continue forty and two months. ... And it was given unto him to make war with the saints, and to overcome them: and power was given him over all kindreds, and tongues, and nations" (Rev. 13:5, 7).

Our next question is simple: When during its forty-two months of world power will the composite beast declare war on the saints? We are not given a date, but let's examine Revelation 11. It reads, "And when they shall have finished their testimony [referring to the two witnesses], the beast that ascendeth out of the bottomless pit [a.k.a. Satan or the eighth beast] shall make war against them, and shall overcome them, and kill them" (Rev. 11:7). When will the two witnesses be killed? Verse 7 says that "when they shall have finished their testimony" they will be killed. Revelation 11:3 says: "They shall prophesy a thousand two hundred and threescore days, clothed in sackcloth." Therefore, we can conclude that the beast from the bottomless pit will declare war against them and kill them when the two witnesses have come to the end of their 1,260 days of "testimony." My conclusion is that the beast will kill the two witnesses at the end of the latter rain. They will die at the end of the 1,260 day vision of Revelation 11:3.

That would explain the reference to the beast from the pit, but when does the composite beast act? John has given us the answer: "And it was *given* unto him to make war with the saints, and to overcome them" (Rev. 13:7, emphasis supplied). In other words, the composite beast will act when he is told to act. This composite beast is part of Babylon. This composite beast will act when the dragon tells it to act. Based on our study of Revelation 11, I believe that the dragon will not act until the 1,260 days of prophecy from the two witnesses have ended. Therefore, the composite beast will act at the end of the forty-two months when the dragon beast acts.

John told us that when these two witnesses finish their presentation of the prophecies of Daniel and Revelation with the power of the latter rain, at the end of the 1,260 days (Rev. 11:3), the beast that will come out of the bottomless pit (a.k.a. Satan) will make war against the two witnesses and kill them.

The composite beast will declare war against "the saints" at the end of the forty-two months or 1,260 days (Rev. 13:5). The beast that ascends out of the bottomless pit will make war against the two witnesses and will kill them at the end of 1,260 days or forty-two months (Rev. 11:2). These two beasts are attacking the same target at the same time. Because of this I believe that this literal 1,260-day time period is the end of the time of the end.

What does John say about this last time period? "But the court which is without the temple leave out, and measure it not; for it is given unto the Gentiles: and the holy city shall they tread under foot forty and two months" (Rev. 11:2). The angel told John that he was not to measure the outer court of the sanctuary of God. That part has been given to the Gentiles. Then the angel gave John an extraordinary prophecy. For forty-two months the Gentiles were to tread under foot the holy city of God. If the holy city is Jerusalem and the timeframe is the end of the time of the end, what could the significance of that statement mean to present-day Israel?

Continuing with the next verse, we read: "And I will give power unto my two witnesses, and they shall prophesy a thousand two hundred and threescore days, clothed in sackcloth (Rev. 11:3). Jesus tells John that He will give the gift of the latter rain of the Holy Spirit to the two witnesses. Then He tells John that these two witnesses will prophecy for 1,260 days. Jesus does not give the date that this prophecy will begin, but He does say how the time period will end. "And when they shall have finished their testimony, the beast that ascendeth out of the bottomless pit shall make war against them, and shall overcome them, and kill them" (Rev. 11:7).

He tells us here that the ministry of the two witnesses will end in three and a half years. The end will be climaxed by the actions of the beast that ascends from the pit. He will come against the two witnesses and kill them. We have studied the identity of this beast. We have determined that the beast that will ascend from the pit at the third coming of Christ is Satan himself (Rev. 20:2, 7). What Satan does in Revelation 11:7 is clearly understood. That is when Satan will declare war against the two witnesses for sharing the prophecies of Daniel and Revelation. This same declaration of war is described in Revelation 12. "And the dragon was wroth with the woman, and went to make war with the remnant of her seed, which keep the commandments of God, and have the testimony of Jesus Christ" (Rev. 12:17).

This timeline of forty-two months, or 1,260 days, is not given in Revelation 12:17, but the goal of the dragon was. He makes war against "the remnant of her seed," which I assume to be the two witnesses, as they finish their testimony at the end of the 1,260-day prophecy. So let's focus on the two time periods in Revelation 11. When we diagram the time periods of the two witnesses we have to begin with the 1,260 days.

The Two Witnesses of Revelation Daniel and John, Begin their work						
Power of Fire	Power of Drought	Power of Water to Blood	Power of Plagues			
1260 Days						

Revelation 11:9 tells us that they were dead for three and a half days, then verse 11 tells us that they were resurrected. Verse 12 tells us that they were then taken to heaven as their enemies watched. We can put these events in a diagram.

The Two Witnesses of Revelation Daniel and John, Begin their work				Killed by the Beast	Raised by the Spirit	Raised to Heaven at the Time of the Earthquake
Power of Fire	Power of Drought	Power of Water to Blood	Power of Plagues			
1260 Days				**3 ½ days**		

Now let's place a diagram of the forty-two months of the time of the Gentiles in parallel with the time diagram of the two witnesses.

Rev. 11:3	"I will give power unto My two witnesses, and they shall prophecy." 1260 Days	Killed by the Beast 3 ½ days	Raised by the Spirit	Raised to Heaven
Rev. 11:2	Gentiles: "The holy city shall they tread underfoot." 42 months			

The prophecy timeline of the two witnesses (Rev. 11:3) parallels the prophecy timeline for the Gentiles (Rev. 11:2). I believe these prophecies will occur at the end of the time of the end. The prophecies were given to John 2,000 years ago. Revelation 11 reveals what the two witnesses will be doing and saying, but what will the Gentiles be doing and saying? In order to understand the actions of the Gentiles, we have to go back to the diagram of Revelation 12 and 13 that we diagramed in the last chapter to see the big picture again.

Revelation 12, 13, and 17

The Woman Rev. 12:1	Woman's last days of pregnancy (12:2)	Woman delivers child, who is called to heaven (12:6)	Woman is in the wilderness for a time, times, and half a time (12:14)		Woman protected as the earth swallows the flood (12:16)	The remnant of the woman's seed (12:17)	**The Eighth Beast** *Given power over the world (13:8) *The world worships the beast
The Red Dragon Rev. 12:3 Spiritualism	4th beast is ready to devour the child (12:4)	4th beast is Pagan Rom and the Devil or Satan	4th beast persecutes the woman (12:13)		4th beast spews a flood out of its mouth to drown the woman (12:15)	**Babylon** 4th beast makes war with the remnant (12:17)	
The Composite Beast Rev. 13:1 Catholicism		4th beast gives 5th beast his power, seat, and authority (13:2)	5th beast receives mortal wound to head (13:3)	5th beast's wound is healed (13:3). The world worships the dragon, which gave power to the beast and the composite beast (13:4)	5th beast is given a mouth to blaspheme God's name, God's temple, God's people for 42 months (13:5–6)	5th beast makes war with the saints (13:7)	
The Lamblike Beast Rev. 13:11 Apostate Protestantism				6th beast commands all the world to worship the composite beast (13:12)	6th beast deceives the people of Earth by miracles and fire (13:13, 14) and commands the Earth to make an image to the beast (13:14, 15)	6th beast gives life to the image of the beast	
The "Image of the Beast" Rev. 13:14						7th beast requires all to wear the mark of the beast or die (13:13–17)	

This diagram below now has a red line down the middle, dividing the historical part, on the left, from the future part, on the right. From the box labeled "Fifth beast's wound is healed (13:3)" (circled in yellow) to the column of the eighth beast are events that we have not yet seen but that God wants us to know about. They will happen right before our eyes.

God tells us that the two witnesses will receive the latter rain, enabling them to warn the world about the judgment of God so they can prepare for the second coming of Jesus, repent, and believe the good news. Like the former rain that fell for three and a half years after the ascension of Jesus, the latter rain will fall for three and a half years. God's timing is exact.

John tells us that the time is coming when spiritualism will come along and heal the wound of Catholicism. This action will so amaze the world that the world will worship spiritualism and Catholicism. The apostate Protestants will ask the world to worship Catholicism. Then John tells us that spiritualism will spew out a flood to try to drown the church of Christ. Catholicism will blaspheme

God for about forty-two months. And apostate Protestantism will be part of the action that will deceive the earth with miracles and fire from heaven.

Then we see the formation of Babylon. Apostate Protestantism will link with Catholicism, who will link with spiritualism. They will come to the point that they must declare war against the children of God. The world will see this when the two witnesses finish their three and a half years of testimony.

The beginning of this prophecy could be when the composite beast gets its wound healed by the pagan Rome beast. So let's use that event to mark the beginning of our timeline. This red line in the middle of the diagram is the beginning of the 1,260-day timeline and extends to the beginning of the eighth beast.

Revelation 12, 13, and 17

The Woman Rev. 12:1	Woman's last days of pregnancy (12:2)	Woman delivers child, who is called to heaven (12:6)	Woman is in the wilderness for a time, times, and half a time (12:14)		Woman protected as the earth swallows the flood (12:16)	The remnant of the woman's seed (12:17)	
The Red Dragon Rev. 12:3 Spiritualism	4th beast is ready to devour the child (12:4)	4th beast is Pagan Rom and the Devil or Satan	4th beast persecutes the woman (12:13)		4th beast spews a flood out of its mouth to drown the woman (12:15)	**Babylon** 4th beast makes war with the remnant (12:17)	**The Eighth Beast** * Given power over the world (13:8) *The world worships the beast
The Composite Beast Rev. 13:1 Catholicism		4th beast gives 5th beast his power, seat, and authority (13:2)	5th beast receives mortal wound to head (13:3)	5th beast's wound is healed (13:3). The world worships the dragon, which gave power to the beast and the composite beast (13:4)	5th beast is given a mouth to blaspheme God's name, God's temple, God's people for 42 months (13:5–6)	5th beast makes war with the saints (13:7)	
The Lamblike Beast Rev. 13:11 Apostate Protestantism				6th beast commands all the world to worship the composite beast (13:12)	6th beast deceives the people of Earth by miracles and fire (13:13, 14) and commands the Earth to make an image to the beast (13:14, 15)	6th beast gives life to the image of the beast	
The "Image of the Beast" Rev. 13:14						7th beast requires all to wear the mark of the beast or die (13:13–17)	

1,260 Days

Revelation 11 tells us about two groups. The two witnesses have 1,260 days to prophesy. The Gentile world has the same amount of time to trample Jerusalem.

This diagram has the timeline that each group was given to John, the witness of Revelation. Would you not think that Daniel, the other witness, would have some idea of this plan? Let's read some verses from Daniel 12 to search for such a revelation:

> And one said to the man clothed in linen, which was upon the waters of the river, How long shall it be to the end of these wonders? And I heard the man clothed in linen, which was upon the waters of the river, when he held up his right hand and his left hand unto heaven, and sware by him that liveth for ever that it shall be for a time, times, and an half; and when he shall have accomplished to scatter the power of the holy people, all these things shall be finished. And I heard, but I understood not: then said I, O my Lord, what shall be the end of these things? And he said, Go thy way, Daniel: for the words are closed up and sealed till the time of the end. Many shall be purified, and made white, and tried; but the wicked shall do wickedly: and none of the wicked shall understand; but the wise shall understand. And from the time that the daily *sacrifice* shall be taken away, and the abomination that maketh desolate set up, there shall be a thousand two hundred and ninety days. Blessed is he that waiteth, and cometh to the thousand three hundred and five and thirty days. (Dan. 12:6–12)

There are three timelines in this dialogue of Daniel 12.

> It shall be for a time, times, and an half; and when he shall have accomplished to scatter the power of the holy people, all these things shall be finished....
> And from the time that the daily *sacrifice* shall be taken away, and the abomination that maketh desolate set up, there shall be a thousand two hundred and ninety days.
> Blessed is he that waiteth, and cometh to the thousand three hundred and five and thirty days. (Dan. 12:7, 11, 12)

When do these timelines begin? Are they consecutive, or are they parallel? Do they have anything to do with the end-time events of Revelation 11 and the 1,260 days of the two witnesses? Chapter 12 tells us that Daniel has been listening to an angel of God describing the world's history in chapter 11. He sees Jesus stand up in the heavenly sanctuary and states that the time of trouble is starting for the world and only those who are written in the Lamb's book of life will be delivered. Then we come to the text quoted above: "And one said to the man clothed in linen, which was upon the waters of the river, How long shall it be to the end of these wonders?" (Dan. 12:6). Jesus gives us the answer in verse 7: "It will be for a time, times and half a time. When the power of the holy people has been finally broken, all these things will be completed" (Dan. 12:7, NIV).

With all the authority and power that He possesses as God, swearing by His own name, lifting up His arms, He tells us that it will finish at the end of "time, times and a half time." This is prophetic language that is equal to three and a half years, or forty-two months, or 1,260 days. Then He tells us that at the end of these 1,260 days, the *power* of the holy people will be shattered and scattered.

I believe that this text of the 1,260 days of Daniel 12:7 is parallel to Revelation 11:7, which says, "And when they [the two witnesses] shall have finished their testimony [at the end of the 1,260 days (Rev. 11:3)], the beast that ascendeth out of the bottomless pit [Satan] shall make war against them, and shall overcome them, and kill them." In other words, when Satan destroys these two witnesses, he will be fulfilling the part of the text that says, "When the power of the holy people has been finally broken" (Dan. 12:7, NLT). Returning to the narrative, we find Daniel asking a question: "And I heard, but I did not understand. Then I said, O my lord, what shall be the issue *and* final end of these things? (Dan. 12:8, AMP)

Then Jesus tells him to go his way. He tells Daniel that the words written in the book of Daniel will be sealed until the end of the world (Dan. 12:9). The righteous will do righteously and the wicked will do wickedly. Then He gives Daniel two more timelines.

> And from the time that the daily sacrifice shall be taken away, and the abomination that maketh desolate set up, there shall be a thousand two hundred and ninety days. Blessed is he that waiteth, and cometh to the thousand three hundred and five and thirty days. (Dan. 12:11, 12)

Jesus tells us that from the time that the daily shall be taken away to the time that the abomination of desolation is established, there will be 1,290 days. Then He gives the best timeline. *Blessed is the man that waits for the 1,335 days.*

Before we continue in our study of the three timelines, we need to understand several phrases. What does the "daily *sacrifice*" and the "abomination of desolation" mean in the second timeline? We need to go to Daniel 8 for the definitions.

> Then I heard one saint speaking, and another saint said unto that certain saint which spake, How long shall be the vision concerning the daily sacrifice, and the transgression of desolation, to give both the sanctuary and the host to be trodden under foot? (Dan. 8:13)

Two heavenly beings are talking to each other in Daniel 8:13, 14. The angel asks: "How long shall be the vision concerning the daily and the transgression of desolation to give both the sanctuary and the host to be trodden under foot?" What is he asking?

In Daniel 8:13, the two adversaries—the daily and the transgression of desolation—are one side of the conflict. The other side is made up of the sanctuary and the host. The adversaries walk all over the sanctuary and the host. The next verse tells us that this will take place for a long time. "And he said unto me, Unto two thousand and three hundred days; then shall the sanctuary be cleansed" (Dan. 8:14).

The sanctuary and the host were to be trodden under foot for 2,300 sanctuary years. At the end of the 2,300 sanctuary years, the sanctuary was to receive a cleansing, putting a stop to the desecration of the adversaries. This cleansing is a reference to the Day of Atonement in the sanctuary year when the Holy and Most Holy Places of the wilderness sanctuary were cleansed by the high priest.

We need to define the characters of each group. The sanctuary is God's spiritual plan of how fallen man would return to his heavenly family. The host represents those who have believed the promises of God and stand at their posts ready for their next command from their Father in heaven. Peter calls them "a royal priesthood" (1 Peter 2:9). So God has given us a picture of His church and those who worship Him.

Thus, if one side represents God's temple and His family, who is on the other side? Would it not be the enemy and his followers? These are the ones who tread under foot the sanctuary and the host. The "daily" represents the false religious system that was seen by Nebuchadnezzar in Daniel 2. We can call that system paganism. Though captivating in brightness and form, this "great image" is the false religious system of the enemy of God. The "transgression of desolation" represents those who have followed this graven image and serve as priests for the enemy of God.

Repeating the question of Daniel 8:13, we read: "How long shall be the vision concerning the daily sacrifice, and the transgression of desolation, to give both the sanctuary and the host to be trodden under foot?" Let us insert our definitions in this text.

> How long shall be the vision concerning the daily [that is, the false religious system of Satan or paganism], and the transgression of desolation [that is, those who have followed this graven image and have served as its priests], to give both the sanctuary [that is, God's spiritual plan of redemption] and the host [that is, those who have followed God] to be trodden under foot? (Dan. 8:13)

In other words, how long will the evil church triumph and trample over God's faithful church? God tells us that for 2,300 sanctuary years, evil will triumph over good. But at the end of that time, God will begin the final cleansing, which is the final judgment. And when that judgment is complete, good will triumph over evil forever.

These definitions from Daniel 8:13, 14 help us understand Daniel 12:11. "And from the time that the daily sacrifice shall be taken away, and the abomination that maketh desolate set up, there shall be a thousand two hundred and ninety days" (Dan. 12:11).

I believe that Jesus is telling us that during this time of 1,290 days (Dan. 12:11) the temple of paganism will be replaced with the abomination of desolation. In other words, the religious system represented by the graven image, seen in Daniel 2 and mentioned in Daniel 12:11, will be replaced with the abomination of desolation. That is to say that this pagan idol will be replaced by the one who made the idol. This abomination is the last great king of the earth. We determined from the diagram in the last chapter that the last king will be the eighth beast of Revelation. His name is Satan. He is the abomination of desolation that will stand in the holy place in Jerusalem (Matt. 24:15).

The good news comes as we look at the third time period in Daniel 12: "Blessed is he that waiteth, and cometh to the thousand three hundred and five and thirty days" (Dan. 12:12).

This is the last time period that Jesus gave Daniel. Whoever endures until the end of this timeline will receive God's blessing. These happy enduring ones will say, "Lo, this is our God; we have waited for him, and he will save us: this is the Lord; we have waited for him, we will be glad and rejoice in his salvation" (Isa. 25:9). That is what it means to be blessed. If you have trusted in Jesus to save you amply, fully, and entirely, you will be looking into heaven and beholding the beauty of our Savior Redeemer in the clouds of heaven at the second coming. That is the blessing God has reserved for His people. If we put all the pieces together, what do the timelines of Revelation 11 look like?

Rev. 11:3	"I will give power unto My two witnesses, and they shall prophecy." 1260 Days	Killed by the Beast 3 ½ days	Raised by the Spirit	Raised to Heaven
Rev. 11:2	Gentiles: "The holy city shall they tread underfoot." 42 months			

How are the timelines of Revelation related to the timelines of Daniel 12? We begin with the 1,260-day timeline. Where should we place the 1,260-day timeline of Daniel 12 in relation to the timelines of Revelation 11? Daniel tells us. The timeline of Daniel 12:7 ends when "the holy people" are scattered or killed by the beast. The timeline of Revelation 11:3–7 ends when the "two witnesses" are killed by the beast. These timelines are parallel. They end with the same event. Therefore, we can put the 1,260-day timeline of Daniel 12:7 next to the timelines from Revelation 11:2, 3.

Rev. 11:3	"I will give power unto My two witnesses, and they shall prophecy." 1260 Days	Killed by the Beast 3 ½ days	Raised by the Spirit	Raised to Heaven
Rev. 11:2	Gentiles: "The holy city shall they tread underfoot." 42 months			
Dan. 12:7	Time: to "scatter the power of the holy people." Times, Times, and ½ Time			

Where then should we place the timeline of the 1,290 days?

| Rev. 11:3 | "I will give power unto My two witnesses, and they shall prophecy." 1260 Days | Killed by the Beast 3 ½ days | Raised by the Spirit | Raised to Heaven |

| Rev. 11:2 | Gentiles: "The holy city shall they tread underfoot." 42 months |

| Dan. 12:7 | Time: to "scatter the power of the holy people." Times, Times, and ½ Time |

| Dan. 12:11 | Time: that "daily shall be removed" and "abomination of desolation" setup 1290 Days |

This last timeline ends when "the daily" is removed and the "abomination of desolation" is set up. Then we come to the last timeline of Daniel 12. Where should we put the timeline of the 1,335 days?

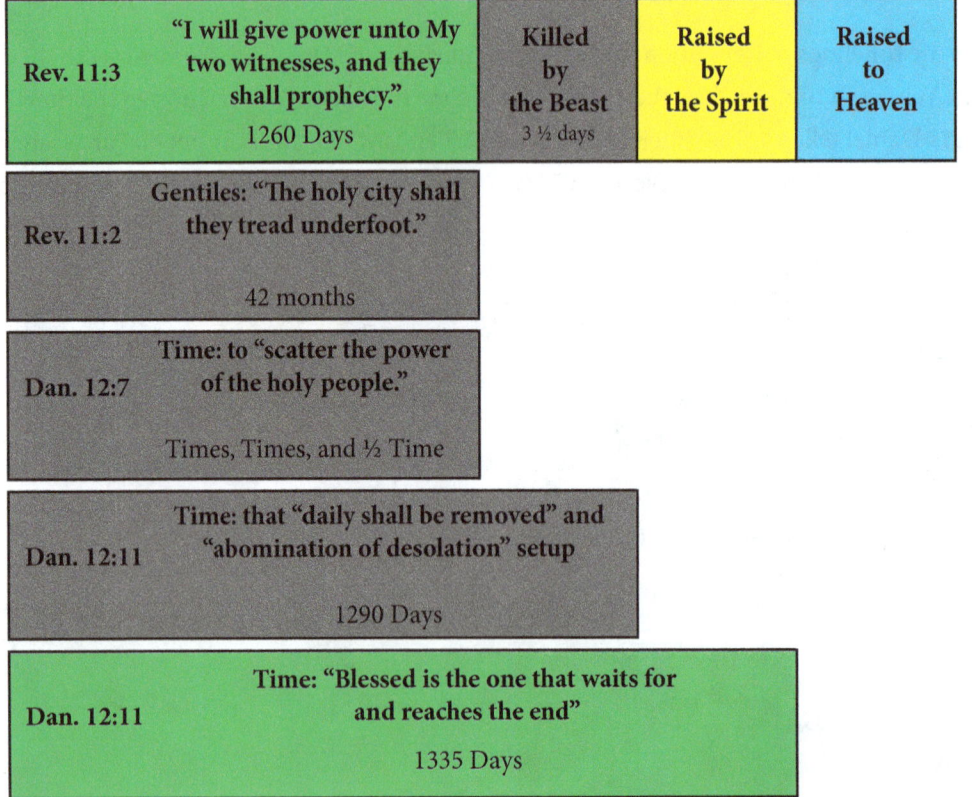

Forty-five days after the establishment of "the abomination of desolation" is the second coming of Jesus Christ. There are more details to add.

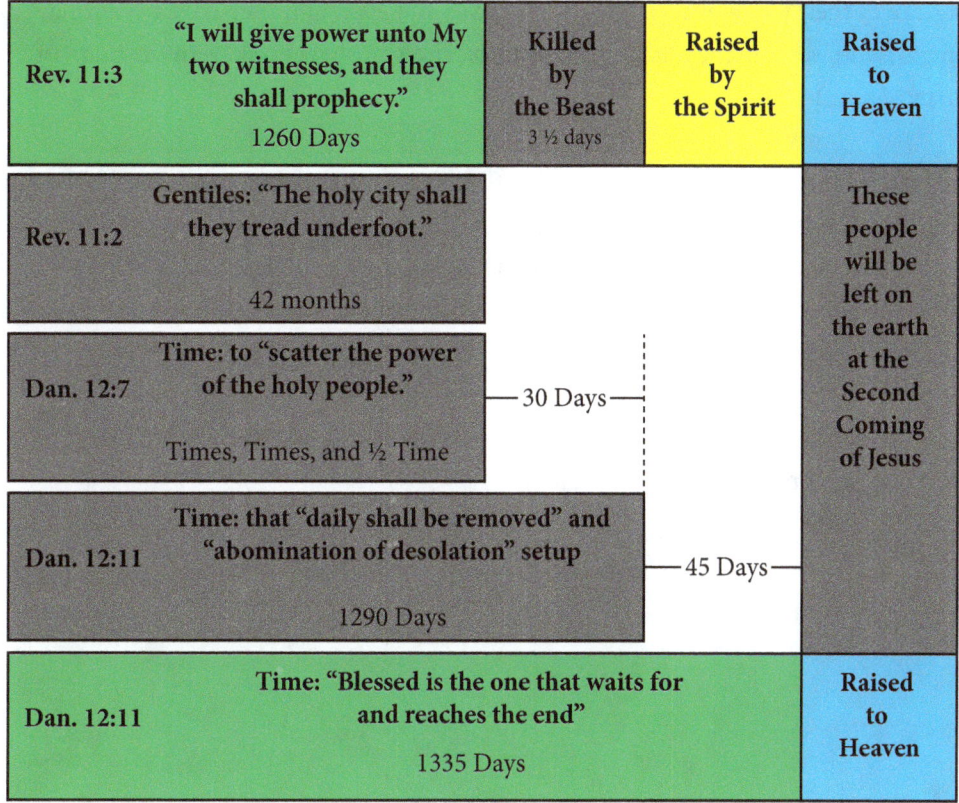

We are looking at end-time events. The world will be separated into two groups. One group will be called blessed and will be raised to heaven. The other group will be destroyed at the second coming of Christ and will be left on the earth.

What advice did Jesus give us when we see the end of the 1,290?

> When ye therefore shall see the abomination of desolation, spoken of by Daniel the prophet, stand in the holy place, (whoso readeth, let him understand:) Then let them which be in Judaea flee into the mountains. (Matt. 24:15, 16)

When you see Satan standing in the holy place in Jerusalem and acting like the Christ of the second coming, they you are to "flee into the mountains." This "abomination of desolation" will capture the attention of the world. This high priest of the false religion is the eighth beast of Revelation 17. As the world watches this grand scene, some will remember the warning from the third angel:

> If any man worship the beast and his image, and receive his mark in his forehead, or in his hand, the same shall drink of the wine of the wrath of God, which is poured out

without mixture into the cup of his indignation; and he shall be tormented with fire and brimstone in the presence of the holy angels, and in the presence of the Lamb: And the smoke of their torment ascendeth up for ever and ever: and they have no rest day nor night, who worship the beast and his image, and whosoever receiveth the mark of his name. (Rev. 14:9–11)

This beast is the eighth beast; we know now that this is non other than Satan himself. The image to the beast is the seventh king, or the new world order, that had power for a short time. Some will have chosen to worship the God of heaven, while others will simply have allowed their senses to be swayed by the grandeur, the beauty, and the musical words from the beast. They will surrender their will and their life to this beast and worship him. And they will be lost.

> "Lord, help us to see what it is that You want us to see. Help us to warn others. Help us to keep our eyes on You."

Chapter 9

Same Enemies, Different Descriptions

The enemies of God operate under many guises. The one thing we know for sure is that they can all be described as wolves in sheep's clothing. We read in Revelation 12 that the red dragon will force on the world its dogma regarding the soul of the individual never dying. The composite beast of Revelation 13 will force on the world its belief that Sunday is sacred and should be observed. A group of apostate Protestants will urge the world to unite in support of spiritualism and Catholicism. The image to the beast will use force to subject the world to its authority and the religious beliefs of Babylon. Revelation 17 introduced us to the eighth and last beast. This eighth beast is the one to which I applied the prophecy of Matthew 24:15 that says that the "abomination of desolation" would stand in "the Holy Place" as the savior of the world. "And all that dwell upon the earth shall worship him, whose names are not written in the book of life of the Lamb slain from the foundation of the world" (Rev. 13:8).

Despite all these enemies of God, Jesus told us that there would be a remnant that would represent Him in the last days of the earth. This last group would become the first. They will "be strong" for God and will "instruct" many. Yet, in the end, they will fall before the destroyer. How can that be? Why would God allow His people to fight for the right and then be overcome?

These same enemies and this same "remnant" of God, who are described in Revelation 12, 13, and 17, are also described in Daniel 11:29–45. We will begin the discussion of these last verses of Daniel 11 by reading about the followers of the Way.

> ... but the people that do know their God shall be strong, and do exploits. And they that understand among the people shall instruct many: yet they shall fall by

the sword, and by flame, by captivity, and by spoil, many days. Now when they shall fall, they shall be holpen with a little help: but many shall cleave to them with flatteries. And some of them of understanding shall fall, to try them, and to purge, and to make them white, even to the time of the end: because it is yet for a time appointed. (Dan. 11:32–35)

Gabriel is describing the vision to Daniel. He comes to the time of the end and tells us that there will be a time when the people of God will be strong, and do deeds, and teach others about God. But in this same narrative he tells us that they will be cast down by "the sword," the "flame," "captivity," and by "spoil" for a time. After their fall, they will be helped to stand again. Some of the faithful will fall from God's group, but the others will be purged and whitened even to the end of the time of the end. These faithful will make it to the appointed time of the second coming of Jesus.

In order for us to understand this group of faithful followers of God in Daniel 11, we must look to the book of Revelation for a parallel. It is found in Revelation 11. Our previous study of this chapter helped us to understand that God has a "standard" to raise against the "flood" of His enemy. That "standard" is seen in the diagram below in the work of the two witnesses.

The Two Witnesses of Revelation Daniel and John, Begin their work				Killed by the Beast	Raised by the Spirit	Raised to Heaven at the Time of the Earthquake
Power of Fire	Power of Drought	Power of Water to Blood	Power of Plagues			
1260 Days				3 ½ days		

Revelation 11 told us that these prophets of God will give a message of warning for the people of the earth at the time of the end. They will be filled with the latter rain from their Father in heaven. They will be strong and they will instruct many, but at the end of their ministry, John is told that they will be killed by the beast that will rise from the bottomless pit. Then Revelation 11 tells us that God will raise them up and carry them to heaven.

This work of the two witnesses was then compared to the timelines of Daniel 12.

Rev. 11:3	"I will give power unto My two witnesses, and they shall prophecy." 1260 Days	Killed by the Beast 3 ½ days	Raised by the Spirit	Raised to Heaven
Rev. 11:2	Gentiles: "The holy city shall they tread underfoot." 42 months			These people will be left on the earth at the Second Coming of Jesus
Dan. 12:7	Time: to "scatter the power of the holy people." Times, Times, and ½ Time	— 30 Days —		
Dan. 12:11	Time: that "daily shall be removed" and "abomination of desolation" setup 1290 Days	— 45 Days —		
Dan. 12:11	Time: "Blessed is the one that waits for and reaches the end" 1335 Days			Raised to Heaven

This comparison, paralleling the timelines of Daniel 12 and the work of the two witnesses in Revelation 11, helped us to visualize and understand the events of the time of the end.

If these three timelines of Daniel 12 can be compared to the events of the people of God in Revelation 11, could they also not be compared to the events of the followers of God in Daniel 11? Let's look at the verses again.

> But the people that do know their God shall be strong, and do exploits. And they that understand among the people shall instruct many: yet they shall fall by the sword, and by flame, by captivity, and by spoil, many days. Now when they shall fall, they shall be holpen with a little help: but many shall cleave to them with flatteries. And some of them of understanding shall fall, to try them, and to purge, and to make them white, even to the time of the end: because it is yet for a time appointed. (Dan. 11:32–35)

Let's try to divide these events into a timeline according to the text in a diagram.

The People that know God v. 32	Shall be strong and do exploits v. 32 Shall instruct many v. 33	Shall fall by sword fire captivity plunder	Helped by a Little Help v. 34 Refined Purified Whitened v. 36	Time of the End The Appointed Time

Daniel 12 has three timelines: the 1,260 days, the 1,290 days, and the 1,335 days. The first one—the 1,260 days (Dan. 12:7, Rev. 11:7)—ends with the death of the two witnesses in Revelation 11, so when we look at the events of Daniel 11 the parallel event would come at the time that they fall by the sword. Let's place that event in our diagram.

		1,260 Days End		
The People that know God v. 32	Shall be strong and do exploits v. 32 Shall instruct many v. 33	Shall fall by sword fire captivity plunder	Helped by a Little Help v. 34 Refined Purified Whitened v. 36	Time of the End The Appointed Time

Since Daniel is told about events that would be seen at the time of the end, we can then conclude that the beginning of the 1,260 days will be seen in the diagram above. Let's place a line there.

1,260 Days Begins		1,260 Days End		
The People that know God v. 32	Shall be strong and do exploits v. 32 Shall instruct many v. 33	Shall fall by sword fire captivity plunder	Helped by a Little Help v. 34 Refined Purified Whitened v. 36	Time of the End The Appointed Time

The next timeline would be the 1,335 days (Dan. 12:12). Since that occurs at "the appointed time," the next diagram is easy to understand.

1,260 Days Begins		1,260 Days End		1,335 Days
The People that know God v. 32	Shall be strong and do exploits v. 32 Shall instruct many v. 33	Shall fall by sword fire captivity plunder	Helped by a Little Help v. 34 Refined Purified Whitened v. 36	Time of the End The Appointed Time

Now it's time for the last timeline from Daniel 12. That would be the timeline of 1,290 days (Dan. 12:11).

1,260 Days Begins		1,260 Days End	1,290 Days	1,335 Days
The People that know God v. 32	Shall be strong and do exploits v. 32 Shall instruct many v. 33	Shall fall by sword fire captivity plunder	Helped by a Little Help v. 34 Refined Purified Whitened v. 36	Time of the End The Appointed Time

The diagram above is the result of comparing the events of the two witnesses in Revelation 11, the timelines of Daniel 12, and the events of "the people that know God" in Daniel 11. Now it's time to look at the rest of the descriptions used by Gabriel in Daniel 11:29–45. We are told that "at the appointed time" we will see events that will tell us that the end of the time of the end is fast approaching.

Let's look at a diagram that we studied earlier.

Revelation 12, 13, and 17

The Woman Rev. 12:1	Woman's last days of pregnancy (12:2)	Woman delivers child, who is called to heaven (12:6)	Woman is in the wilderness for a time, times, and half a time (12:14)		Woman protected as the earth swallows the flood (12:16)	The remnant of the woman's seed (12:17)	
The Red Dragon Rev. 12:3 **Spiritualism**	4th beast is ready to devour the child (12:4)	4th beast is Pagan Rom and the Devil or Satan	4th beast persecutes the woman (12:13)		4th beast spews a flood out of its mouth to drown the woman (12:15)	**Babylon** 4th beast makes war with the remnant (12:17)	**The Eighth Beast** * Given power over the world (13:8) *The world worships the beast
The Composite Beast Rev. 13:1 **Catholicism**		4th beast gives 5th beast his power, seat, and authority (13:2)	5th beast receives mortal wound to head (13:3)	5th beast's wound is healed (13:3). The world worships the dragon, which gave power to the beast and the composite beast (13:4)	5th beast is given a mouth to blaspheme God's name, God's temple, God's people for 42 months (13:5–6)	5th beast makes war with the saints (13:7)	
The Lamblike Beast Rev. 13:11 **Apostate Protestantism**				6th beast commands all the world to worship the composite beast (13:12)	6th beast deceives the people of Earth by miracles and fire (13:13, 14) and commands the Earth to make an image to the beast (13:14, 15)	6th beast gives life to the image of the beast	
The "Image of the Beast" Rev. 13:14						7th beast requires all to wear the mark of the beast or die (13:13–17)	

1,260 Days

This diagram represents the parallel actions of the woman's seed, the red dragon, the composite beast, the lamblike beast, the image to the beast, and the eighth beast described in Revelation 12, 13, and 17. What should be obvious is that in the time period marked 1,260 days, all these characters have a role to play at the time of the end.

When we studied this concept in Revelation 12 and 13, we noted that each successive power was in parallel to the woman and the red dragon. Now that we are in Daniel 11, we will find that this clear and logical concept of parallel actions in Revelation 12, 13 and 17 will not be found in Daniel 11, but we will find that each player mentioned in Revelation 12, 13, and 17 can be seen in Daniel 11.

So let us begin by diagramming the foundation of the "appointed time." It will have the same events we just organized according to the three timelines of Revelation 12.

Same Enemies, Different Descriptions

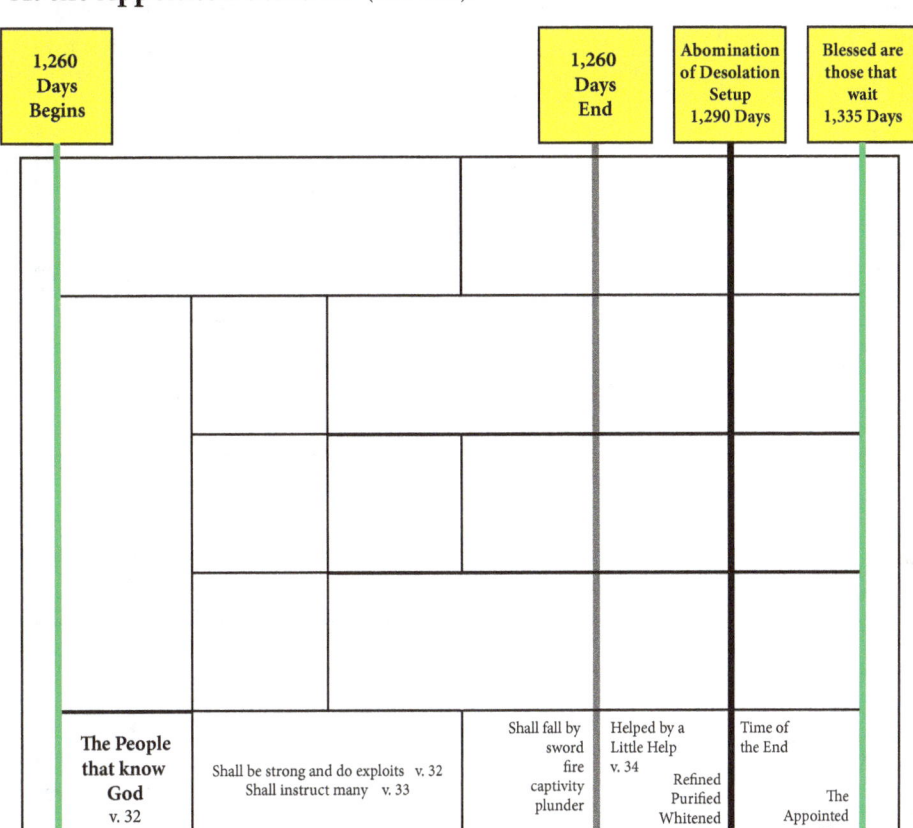

To this basic diagram we will add each description given by Gabriel. We begin with Daniel 11:29–32.

At the time appointed he shall return, and come toward the south; but it shall not be as the former, or as the latter. For the ships of Chittim shall come against him: therefore he shall be grieved, and return, and have indignation against the holy covenant: so shall he do; he shall even return, and have intelligence with them that forsake the holy covenant. And arms shall stand on his part, and they shall pollute the sanctuary of strength, and shall take away the daily *sacrifice*, and they shall place the abomination that maketh desolate. And such as do wickedly against the covenant shall he corrupt by flatteries. (Dan. 11:29–32)

What an incredible vision in so few words. The most notable is in verse 31. An army will stand for the king of the North and he will remove the daily, the enemy's system of pagan worship, and in its place he will put "the abomination" of desolation. This is easy to insert in this diagram. We will place this "abomination of desolation set up" right in front of the 1,290 timeline.

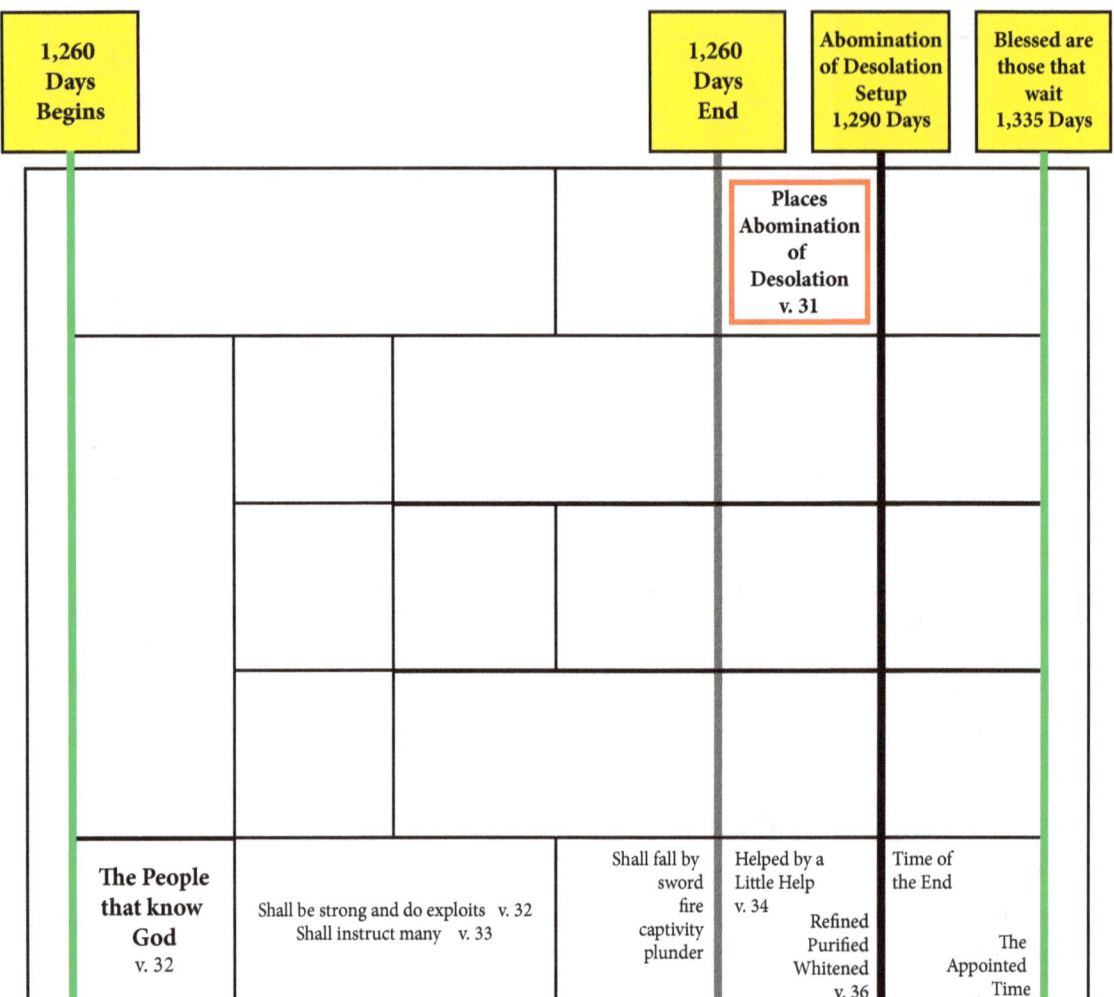

The standing army and the removing of the system of paganism should then be placed in the box to the left of the "abomination of desolation."

"At the Appointed Time ..." (Dan. 11:29).

1,260 Days Begins			1,260 Days End	Abomination of Desolation Setup 1,290 Days	Blessed are those that wait 1,335 Days
			An Army stands Violation of Sanctuary of Strength Daily Stopped v. 31	Places Abomination of Desolation v. 31	
The People that know God v. 32	Shall be strong and do exploits v. 32 Shall instruct many v. 33		Shall fall by sword fire captivity plunder	Helped by a Little Help v. 34 Refined Purified Whitened v. 36	Time of the End

The Appointed Time |

Next we should place Daniel 11:29, 30 in the box to the left of the works of the army.

"At the Appointed Time ..." (Dan. 11:29).

1,260 Days Begins			1,260 Days End	Abomination of Desolation Setup 1,290 Days	Blessed are those that wait 1,335 Days
	The King of the North returns v. 29 Ships of Chittim against him v. 30 King of the North humiliated, retreats Angry toward Holy Covenant **Conspires against Holy Covenant**		An Army stands Violation of Sanctuary of Strength Daily Stopped v. 31	Places Abomination of Desolation v. 31	
The People that know God v. 32	Shall be strong and do exploits v. 32 Shall instruct many v. 33		Shall fall by sword fire captivity plunder	Helped by a Little Help v. 34 Refined Purified Whitened v. 36	Time of the End The Appointed Time

The diagram helps us to understand the relationship between a worldly power and the people of God. Gabriel told us that this power will have a part in placing "the abomination of desolation" in world history. We can now see that with the diagram above. Then, right before this occurs, this power will remove the system of paganism that has been the poster child of the enemy of God. That will be another major move by God's enemy. Then we see in the red rectangle that this power will conspire against the holy covenant. Is this the time that the enemy of God will elevate Sunday as a solution for the world's problems, and thereby make it sacred? Will they then pass a law that this false Sabbath must be worshipped for the good of mankind? Could be, but what is amazing is that these two events, mentioned in Daniel 11, are mentioned by the first two timelines of Daniel 12.

Daniel 12:7 tells us that at the end of the 1,260, "he shall have accomplished to scatter the power of the holy people." Then the second timeline, the 1,290, "the abomination of desolation" (Dan. 12:11) will be set up. We are looking at prophetic timelines from God. He is warning us and appealing to us to get ready.

Let us look at the next verse: "And the king shall do according to his will; and he shall exalt himself, and magnify himself above every god, and shall speak marvellous things against the God of gods, and shall prosper till the indignation be accomplished: for that that is determined shall be done" (Dan. 11:36).

Daniel is told that this next power will show himself. This "king" has a strong will. He will exalt himself and blaspheme God. He will prosper until "the indignation," "the abomination of desolation," will be set. We can put him in the diagram:

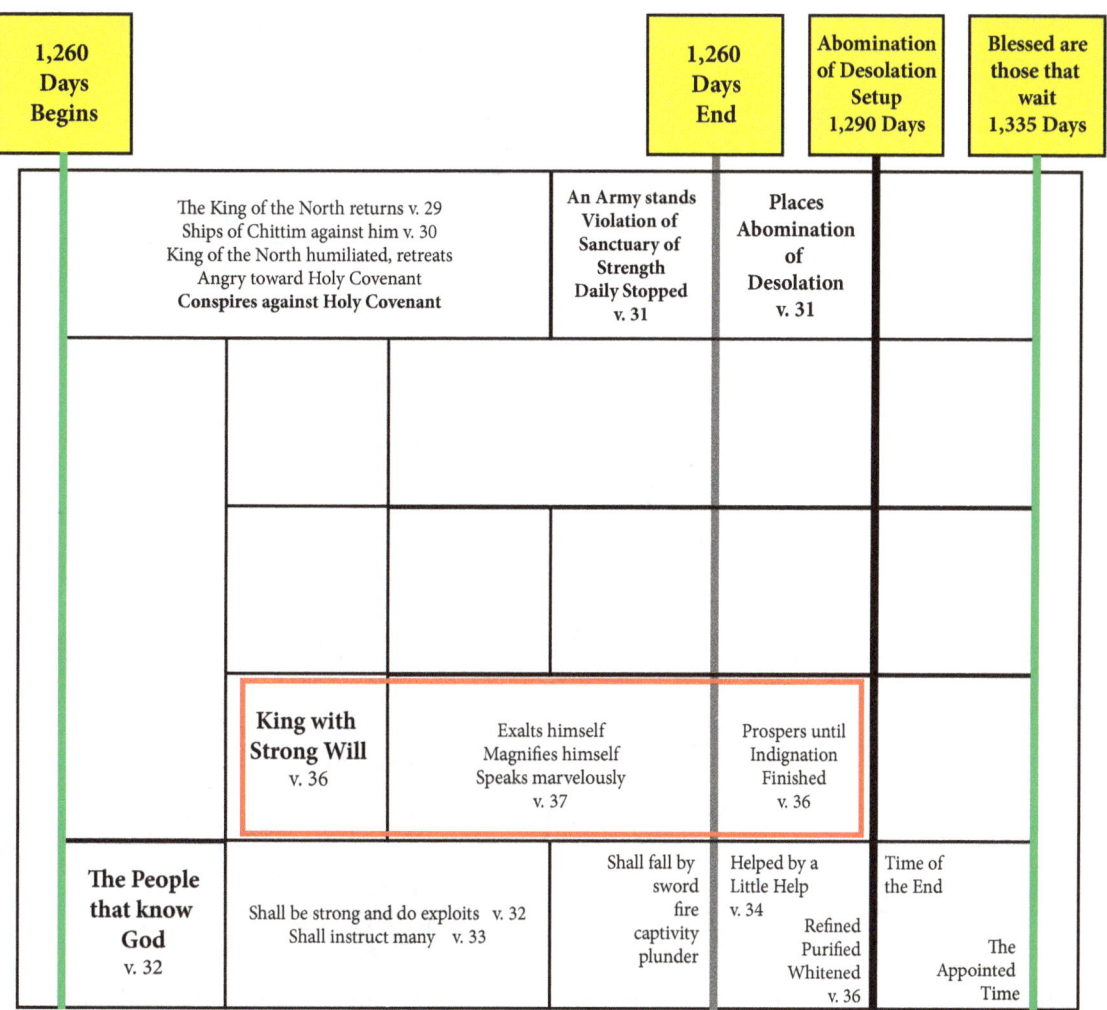

This king with "the strong will" is seen in the diagram above. Gabriel tells us that he will exalt and magnify himself. He will prosper until the indignation is finished or the "abomination of desolation" is set up before the world to be worshiped. Then we come to the next power: "But in his estate shall he honour the God of forces: and a god whom his fathers knew not shall he honour with gold, and silver, and with precious stones, and pleasant things" (Dan. 11:38).

Gabriel tells us that this new power will be called the "god of forces," or the god of war. This power will be new. He will be a power that has not been seen before by the world. He will be motivated, not by principle, but by gold, silver, and diamonds.

We will add him to the diagram. This god of war will be seen again in the narrative of Gabriel.

"At the Appointed Time ..." (Dan. 11:29).

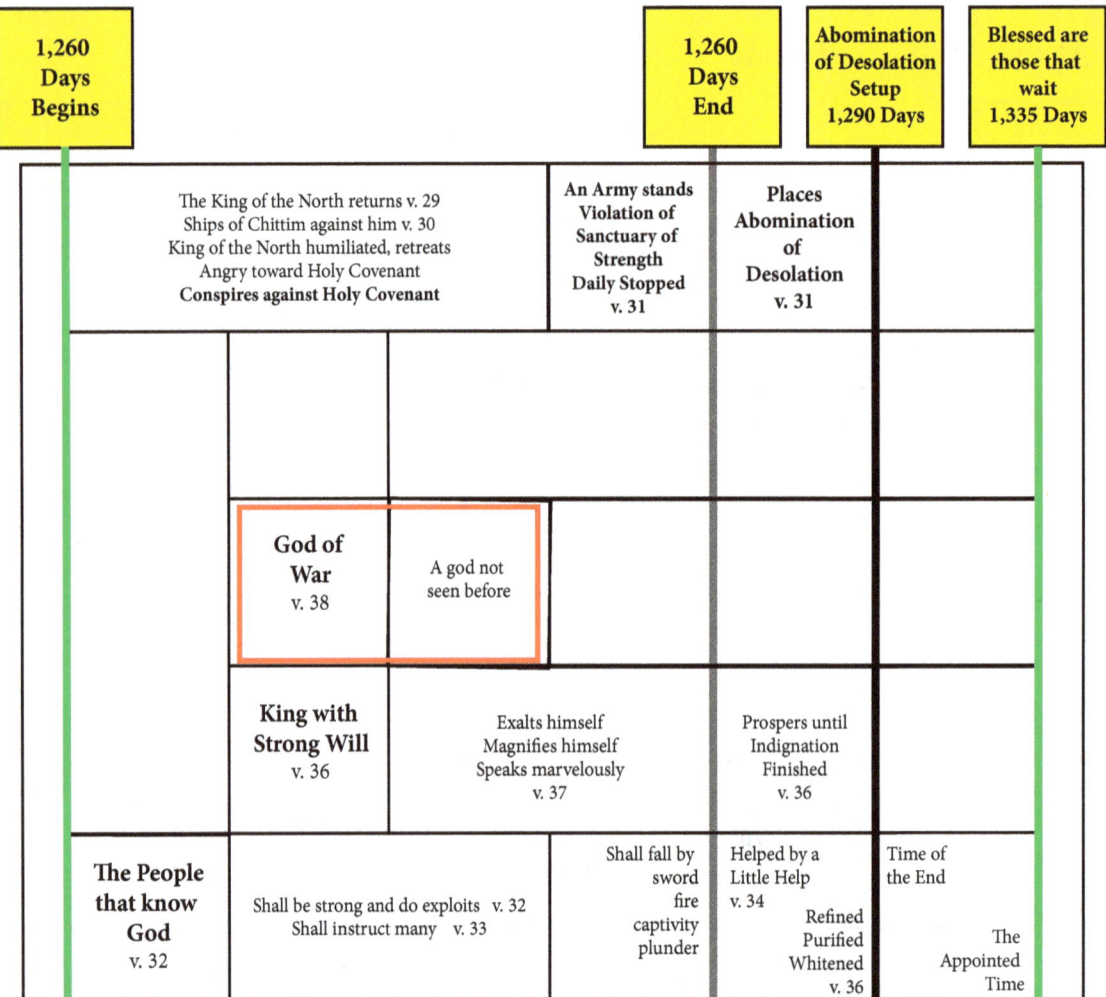

Now let us look at the last power mentioned by Gabriel in Daniel 11: "Thus shall he do in the most strong holds with a strange god, whom he shall acknowledge and increase with glory: and he shall cause them to rule over many, and shall divide the land for gain" (Dan. 11:39).

This last beast is called "a strange god." The king of the North will acknowledge this "strange god" before the leaders of the world. He will then glorify this "strange god" before the people of the world.

This "strange god" will be given the right to rule over the world.

We can add him to our diagram. He will be seen again in Gabriel's narrative.

"At the Appointed Time …" (Dan. 11:29).

1,260 Days Begins			1,260 Days End	Abomination of Desolation Setup 1,290 Days	Blessed are those that wait 1,335 Days
	The King of the North returns v. 29 Ships of Chittim against him v. 30 King of the North humiliated, retreats Angry toward Holy Covenant **Conspires against Holy Covenant**		An Army stands Violation of Sanctuary of Strength Daily Stopped v. 31	Places Abomination of Desolation v. 31	
	The Strange God v. 39	Acknowledged Glorified Give Rule and Divided Land			
	God of War v. 38	A god not seen before			
	King with Strong Will v. 36	Exalts himself Magnifies himself Speaks marvelously v. 37		Prospers until Indignation Finished v. 36	
The People that know God v. 32	Shall be strong and do exploits v. 32 Shall instruct many v. 33		Shall fall by sword fire captivity plunder	Helped by a Little Help v. 34 Refined Purified Whitened v. 36	Time of the End The Appointed Time

Are you beginning to see what is going on in this diagram. Just like you saw in the diagram from Revelation 12, 13, and 17, we are starting to see that there are multiple players on the side of the enemy and only one on the side of God. There are multiple influential ways and various dogmas that will be thrown on the consciousness of the people of the world. But God's way is clear and full of truth—it can be trusted and relied upon. You can trust your life with God's word and way.

Let's finish this section.

> And at the time of the end shall the king of the south push at him: and the king of the north shall come against him like a whirlwind, with chariots, and with horsemen, and with many ships; and he shall enter into the countries, and shall overflow and pass over.

He shall enter also into the glorious land, and many countries shall be overthrown: but these shall escape out of his hand, even Edom, and Moab, and the chief of the children of Ammon. He shall stretch forth his hand also upon the countries: and the land of Egypt shall not escape. But he shall have power over the treasures of gold and of silver, and over all the precious things of Egypt: and the Libyans and the Ethiopians shall be at his steps. But tidings out of the east and out of the north shall trouble him: therefore he shall go forth with great fury to destroy, and utterly to make away many. (Dan. 11:40–44)

There is a lot happening in these verses. Let's break this into manageable pieces: "And at the time of the end shall the king of the south push at him: and the king of the north shall come against him like a whirlwind, with chariots, and with horsemen, and with many ships; and he shall enter into the countries, and shall overflow and pass over. He shall enter also into the glorious land" (Dan. 11:40).

Gabriel tells us that at the time of the end the king of the north, or the "god of war," will come against "the king of the south." He will do this like a whirlwind with a great army, and he will be victorious. Then he will enter the "glorious land." Let's put this information in the diagram.

"At the Appointed Time ..." (Dan. 11:29).

			1,260 Days Begins		1,260 Days End	Abomination of Desolation Setup 1,290 Days	Blessed are those that wait 1,335 Days
	The King of the North returns v. 29 Ships of Chittim against him v. 30 King of the North humiliated, retreats Angry toward Holy Covenant **Conspires against Holy Covenant**			An Army stands Violation of Sanctuary of Strength Daily Stopped v. 31	Places Abomination of Desolation v. 31		
	The Strange God v. 39	Acknowledged Glorified Give Rule and Divided Land					
	God of War v. 38	A god not seen before	Tme of End Whirlwind Glorious land v. 40				
	King with Strong Will v. 36	Exalts himself Magnifies himself Speaks marvelously v. 37			Prospers until Indignation Finished v. 36		
The People that know God v. 32	Shall be strong and do exploits v. 32 Shall instruct many v. 33			Shall fall by sword fire captivity plunder	Helped by a Little Help v. 34 Refined Purified Whitened v. 36	Time of the End The Appointed Time	

Then we learn that this "god of war" has power over men and money: "... with chariots, and with horsemen, and with many ships; and he shall enter into the countries, and shall overflow and pass over. He shall enter also into the glorious land, and many countries shall be overthrown: ... He shall stretch forth his hand also upon the countries: and the land of Egypt shall not escape. But he shall have power over the treasures of gold and of silver, and over all the precious things of Egypt" (Dan. 11:40).

Let's put that in our diagram.

"At the Appointed Time ..." (Dan. 11:29).

1,260 Days Begins			1,260 Days End	Abomination of Desolation Setup 1,290 Days	Blessed are those that wait 1,335 Days
	The King of the North returns v. 29 Ships of Chittim against him v. 30 King of the North humiliated, retreats Angry toward Holy Covenant **Conspires against Holy Covenant**		An Army stands Violation of Sanctuary of Strength Daily Stopped v. 31	Places Abomination of Desolation v. 31	
	The Strange God v. 39	Acknowledged Glorified Give Rule and Divided Land			
	God of War v. 38	A god not seen before	Time of End Wirlwind Glorious land v. 40	Chariots Horsemen Ships v. 43 Power over Silver and Gold	
	King with Strong Will v. 36		Exalts himself Magnifies himself Speaks marvelously v. 37	Prospers until Indignation Finished v. 36	
The People that know God v. 32	Shall be strong and do exploits v. 32 Shall instruct many v. 33		Shall fall by sword fire captivity plunder	Helped by a Little Help v. 34 Refined Purified Whitened v. 36	Time of the End The Appointed Time

Then Gabriel says that this "god of war" will try to destroy many: "… and the Libyans and the Ethiopians shall be at his steps. But tidings out of the east and out of the north shall trouble him: therefore he shall go forth with great fury to destroy, and utterly to make away many" (Dan. 11:43, 44).

Even though this "god of war" has a great army, he will have the problem of the Libyans and Ethiopians nipping at his heels. Gabriel next says that this powerful "god of war" will hear news from the east and out of the north that will trouble his heart. He will respond with anger and a determined effort to destroy his enemies.

"At the Appointed Time …" (Dan. 11:29).

			1,260 Days Begins			**1,260 Days End**	**Abomination of Desolation Setup 1,290 Days**	**Blessed are those that wait 1,335 Days**
			The King of the North returns v. 29 Ships of Chittim against him v. 30 King of the North humiliated, retreats Angry toward Holy Covenant **Conspires against Holy Covenant**			An Army stands Violation of Sanctuary of Strength Daily Stopped v. 31	Places Abomination of Desolation v. 31	
				The Strange God v. 39	Acknowledged Glorified Give Rule and Divided Land			
				God of War v. 38	A god not seen before	Time of End Wirlwind Glorious land v. 40	Chariots Horsemen Ships v. 43 Power over Silver and Gold	Tidings from East v. 44 Fury of Destruction
				King with Strong Will v. 36		Exalts himself Magnifies himself Speaks marvelously v. 37	Prospers until Indignation Finished v. 36	
			The People that know God v. 32	Shall be strong and do exploits v. 32 Shall instruct many v. 33		Shall fall by sword fire captivity plunder	Helped by a Little Help v. 34 Refined Purified Whitened v. 36	Time of the End The Appointed Time

This "god of war" will come out like a "whirlwind." He will come to control the world's gold and silver and will go out at the final minute like a "fury of destruction." Then, one of the powers will make his home near Jerusalem. Yet, he will helplessly come to his end: "And he shall plant the tabernacles of his palace between the seas in the glorious holy mountain; yet he shall come to his end, and none shall help him" (Dan. 11:45). So where should this identifying characteristic be placed in the diagram of Daniel 11?

"At the Appointed Time …" (Dan. 11:29).

1,260 Days Begins				1,260 Days End	Abomination of Desolation Setup 1,290 Days	Blessed are those that wait 1,335 Days
		The King of the North returns v. 29 Ships of Chittim against him v. 30 King of the North humiliated, retreats Angry toward Holy Covenant **Conspires against Holy Covenant**		An Army stands Violation of Sanctuary of Strength Daily Stopped v. 31	Places Abomination of Desolation v. 31	
	The Strange God v. 39	Acknowledged Glorified Give Rule and Divided Land			Plants his Palace v. 45	Comes to his End
	God of War v. 38	A god not seen before	Time of End Wirlwind Glorious land v. 40		Chariots Horsemen Ships v. 43 Power over Silver and Gold	Tidings from East v. 44 Fury of Destruction
	King with Strong Will v. 36	Exalts himself Magnifies himself Speaks marvelously v. 37			Prospers until Indignation Finished v. 36	
The People that know God v. 32		Shall be strong and do exploits v. 32 Shall instruct many v. 33		Shall fall by sword fire captivity plunder	Helped by a Little Help v. 34 Refined Purified Whitened v. 36	Time of the End The Appointed Time

    The next verse adds the final piece to the diagram: "And at that time shall Michael stand up, the great prince which standeth for the children of thy people: and there shall be a time of trouble, such as never was since there was a nation even to that same time: and at that time thy people shall be delivered, every one that shall be found written in the book" (Dan. 12:1).

    When the world seems ready to enter into a war that will destroy many, Gabriel says that our High Priest in the heavenly sanctuary will stand for us and the time of trouble will begin. At long last, we will look up and see the second coming of Jesus. Blessed are those who wait for the second coming of Jesus, which marks the end of the reign of sin on this earth and the beginning of life with our Savior. The second coming of Jesus is the hope and prayer of everyone who believes that Jesus can save us amply, fully, and entirely.

    So who are these powers? From our application of Daniel 11 in this diagram, we have concluded that there will be a struggle between the powers of evil and the children of God. We saw this same

Same Enemies, Different Descriptions

struggle when we studied Revelation 12 and 13. These two chapters revealed that the church of God will be persecuted by the red dragon (pagan Rome or spiritualism), the composite beast (papal Rome or Catholicism), the lamblike beast (apostate Protestantism working through the United States of America), the image to the beast (the new world order), and the eighth beast (Satan himself). So why go through this list again? It is because the list is parallel with the powers seen in Daniel 11. Let's identify these powers in our diagram.

"At the Appointed Time …" (Dan. 11:29).

1,260 Days Begins			1,260 Days End	Abomination of Desolation Setup 1,290 Days	Blessed are those that wait 1,335 Days
	The King of the North returns v. 29 Ships of Chittim against him v. 30 King of the North humiliated, retreats Angry toward Holy Covenant **Conspires against Holy Covenant**		An Army stands Violation of Sanctuary of Strength Daily Stopped v. 31	Places Abomination of Desolation v. 31	
	The Strange God v. 39	Acknowledged Glorified Give Rule and Divided Land		Plants his Palace v. 45	Comes to his End
	God of War v. 38	A god not seen before	Time of End Wirlwind Glorious land v. 40	Chariots Horsemen Ships v. 43 Power over Silver and Gold	Tidings from East v. 44 Fury of Destruction
	King with Strong Will v. 36	Exalts himself Magnifies himself Speaks marvelously v. 37		Prospers until Indignation Finished v. 36	
The People that know God v. 32	Shall be strong and do exploits v. 32 Shall instruct many v. 33		Shall fall by sword fire captivity plunder	Helped by a Little Help v. 34 Refined Purified Whitened v. 36	Time of the End The Appointed Time

"The people that know God" are easy to identify. They have an order from their king: "Go ye therefore, and teach all nations …" (Matt 28:19). That is their calling in this description in Daniel 11.

"The king with a strong will" is also easy to identify. Daniel tells us that he will exalt himself and magnify himself. When we compare these characteristics with the beast of Revelation 13, we discover that this strong-willed power in Daniel 11 is like the composite beast (papal Rome) of Revelation 13.

That leaves us with four more beasts from Revelation 12 and 13 to match with the powers of Daniel 11.

- The Red Dragon (Pagan Rome or Spiritualism)
- The Lamblike Beast (Apostate Protestantism working through the United States of America)
- The Image to the Beast (the New World Order)
- The Eighth Beast (Satan himself)

"The god of war" is the beast that will war against those who do not worship the beast and his image. This is a description of the image to the beast (the new world order).

"The strange god" is a bit complex. He begins as the red dragon, or spiritualism, but he is really the eighth beast, or Satan, because Satan is the one who has the goal of planting "the tabernacles of his palace between the seas in the glorious holy mountain" (Dan. 11:45).

That leaves us one beast to identify:

> For the ships of Chittim shall come against him: therefore he shall be grieved, and return, and have indignation against the holy covenant: so shall he do; he shall even return, and have intelligence with them that forsake the holy covenant. And arms shall stand on his part, and they shall pollute the sanctuary of strength, and shall take away the daily *sacrifice*, and they shall place the abomination that maketh desolate. And such as do wickedly against the covenant shall he corrupt by flatteries: but the people that do know their God shall be strong, and do exploits. (Dan. 11:30–32)

By process of elimination, we can correlate this description with the lamblike beast of Revelation 13, which symbolizes apostate Protestantism working through the United States of America. Thus, the text tells us that "the ships of Chittim" will come against the United States of America and defeat them. Then we are told that the United States of America will return in anger against "the holy covenant." This country will even come to the point at which it will work with those who forsake the covenant of God.

This narrative then tells us that the activities of the time of the end will occur right before our eyes: "And arms shall stand on his part, and they shall pollute the sanctuary of strength, and shall take away the daily *sacrifice*, and they shall place the abomination that maketh desolate" (Dan. 11:31).

An army will stand on the side of the United States of America. This union of Babylon and the image to the beast will use its power and force to supplant idolatry ["the daily"]. Then they will place the "abomination of desolation" in the holy place in Jerusalem. As stated previously, I believe this "abomination of desolation" is Satan standing in the holy place in Jerusalem.

Same Enemies, Different Descriptions

Let's put this new information into our diagram from Daniel 11 to see what it says.

"At the Appointed Time ..." (Dan. 11:29).

1,260 Days Begins			1,260 Days End	Abomination of Desolation Setup 1,290 Days	Blessed are those that wait 1,335 Days
The Lamb like Beast	The King of the North returns v. 29 Ships of Chittim against him v. 30 King of the North humiliated, retreats Angry toward Holy Covenant **Conspires against Holy Covenant**		An Army stands Violation of Sanctuary of Strength Daily Stopped v. 31	Places Abomination of Desolation v. 31	
The Eighth Beast	**The Strange God** v. 39	Acknowledged Glorified Give Rule and Divided Land		Plants his Palace v. 45	Comes to his End
Image to the Beast	**God of War** v. 38	A god not seen before	Time of End Wirlwind Glorious land v. 40	Chariots Horsemen Ships v. 43 Power over Silver and Gold	Tidings from East v. 44 Fury of Destruction
Composite Beast	**King with Strong Will** v. 36	Exalts himself Magnifies himself Speaks marvelously v. 37		Prospers until Indignation Finished v. 36	
The People that know God v. 32	Shall be strong and do exploits v. 32 Shall instruct many v. 33		Shall fall by sword fire captivity plunder	Helped by a Little Help v. 34 Refined Purified Whitened v. 36	Time of the End The Appointed Time

Now, let's contrast this diagram with the one from Revelation 12, 13, and 17.

Revelation 12, 13, and 17

The Woman Rev. 12:1	Woman's last days of pregnancy (12:2)	Woman delivers child, who is called to heaven (12:6)	Woman is in the wilderness for a time, times, and half a time (12:14)		Woman protected as the earth swallows the flood (12:16)	The remnant of the woman's seed (12:17)	
The Red Dragon Rev. 12:3 Spiritualism	4th beast is ready to devour the child (12:4)	4th beast is Pagan Rom and the Devil or Satan	4th beast persecutes the woman (12:13)		4th beast spews a flood out of its mouth to drown the woman (12:15)	**Babylon** 4th beast makes war with the remnant (12:17)	**The Eighth Beast** *Given power over the world (13:8) *The world worships the beast
The Composite Beast Rev. 13:1 Catholicism	4th beast gives 5th beast his power, seat, and authority (13:2)	5th beast receives mortal wound to head (13:3)	5th beast's wound is healed (13:3). The world worships the dragon, which gave power to the beast and the composite beast (13:4)	5th beast is given a mouth to blaspheme God's name, God's temple, God's people for 42 months (13:5-6)	5th beast makes war with the saints (13:7)		
The Lamblike Beast Rev. 13:11 Apostate Protestantism			6th beast commands all the world to worship the composite beast (13:12)	6th beast deceives the people of Earth by miracles and fire (13:13, 14) and commands the Earth to make an image to the beast (13:14, 15)	6th beast gives life to the image of the beast		
The "Image of the Beast" Rev. 13:14					7th beast requires all to wear the mark of the beast or die (13:13-17)		

1,260 Days

The details of Daniel 11 are slightly different from those of Revelation 12 and 13, but the players are the same. I believe that God is giving us a big picture of the end of the time of the end through His two witnesses, Daniel and John. Let's consider this warning from Jesus:

> And this gospel of the kingdom shall be preached in all the world for a witness unto all nations; and then shall the end come. When ye therefore shall see the abomination of desolation, spoken of by Daniel the prophet, stand in the holy place, (whoso readeth, let him understand:) Then let them which be in Judaea flee into the mountains: (Matt. 24:14–16)

Jesus tells us that right after the two witnesses end their work at the end of the 1,260 days, the good news of the gospel of the kingdom will come to an end. The whole world will witness that event, and they will witness "the abomination of desolation" standing in the holy place of the sanctuary in Jerusalem. When Christ's faithful followers see this, they are to flee into the mountains for the time of trouble will begin. Jesus tells us what will happen after this time of trouble.

> Immediately after the tribulation of those days shall the sun be darkened, and the moon shall not give her light, and the stars shall fall from heaven, and the powers of the heavens shall be shaken: And then shall appear the sign of the Son of man in heaven: and then shall all the tribes of the earth mourn, and they shall see the Son of man coming in the clouds of heaven with power and great glory. And he shall send his angels with a great sound of a trumpet, and they shall gather together his elect from the four winds, from one end of heaven to the other. (Matt. 24:29–31)

After the great tribulation, Jesus will come in the clouds of heaven. His trumpet will sound, and His angels will gather all His children from the four corners of the earth. God reveals His secret things to His children that we might prepare for the last battle with the enemy of God.

> The secret *things belong* unto the LORD our God: but those *things which are* revealed *belong* unto us and to our children for ever, that *we* may do all the words of this law. (Deut. 29:29)

If we are to follow the words of the law as seen in Revelation, we must study them that we might show ourselves approved of God, and we must warn our families, our neighbors, and the rest of the world.

> "Thank you, Father, for the two witnesses of Daniel and John. Thank you, Father, that we might glimpse the future through their eyes. Help us, Father, to tell others of this great mystery."

Chapter 10
Victory Assured!

Daniel was shown Satan's demise: "And he said, Behold, I will make thee know what shall be in the last end of the indignation: for at the time appointed the end shall be. The ram which thou sawest having two horns are the kings of Media and Persia. And the rough goat is the king of Grecia: and the great horn that is between his eyes is the first king" (Dan. 8:19–21).

Gabriel is explaining the vision of Daniel 8 to the prophet. He says that he will tell Daniel the events that will occur at the very end of time. Then he recounts the vision: *The ram that you saw in the vision represents the country of Medo-Persia. The goat is the country of Greece.* We know from our previous studies that Babylon was the first king, Medo-Persia was the second, and Greece was the third. Then Gabriel said that there would be four other kings. "Now that being broken, whereas four stood up for it, four kingdoms shall stand up out of the nation, but not in his power" (Dan. 8:22).

After Babylon, Medo-Persia, Greece, and pagan and papal Rome came the United States of America and the new world order. We numbered pagan Rome as the fourth king, papal Rome as the fifth, the United States of America as the sixth, and new world order as the seventh. Then Daniel is told about the eighth king:

> And in the latter time of their kingdom, when the transgressors are come to the full, a king of fierce countenance, and understanding dark sentences, shall stand up. And his power shall be mighty, but not by his own power: and he shall destroy wonderfully, and shall prosper, and practice, and shall destroy the mighty and the holy people. And through his policy also he shall cause craft to prosper in his hand; and he shall magnify himself in his heart, and by peace shall destroy many: he shall also stand up against the Prince of princes; but he shall be broken without hand. (Dan. 8:23–25)

Gabriel tells Daniel that at the end of the time of the end Satan "shall stand up" and be given power from Babylon and from the image of the beast. He will destroy wonderfully. He will prosper and practice. Next is the key phrase: He "shall destroy the mighty and the holy people." This destruction of the "mighty and holy people" is the same vision that John was given in Revelation 11:7: "And when they shall have finished their testimony, the beast that ascendeth out of the bottomless pit shall make war against them, and shall overcome them, and kill them."

Victory Assured!

When the two witnesses finish their testimony at the end of the 1,260 years, Satan will make war with them and overcome and kill them. Do you remember the diagram that compared Revelation 11 with Daniel 12?

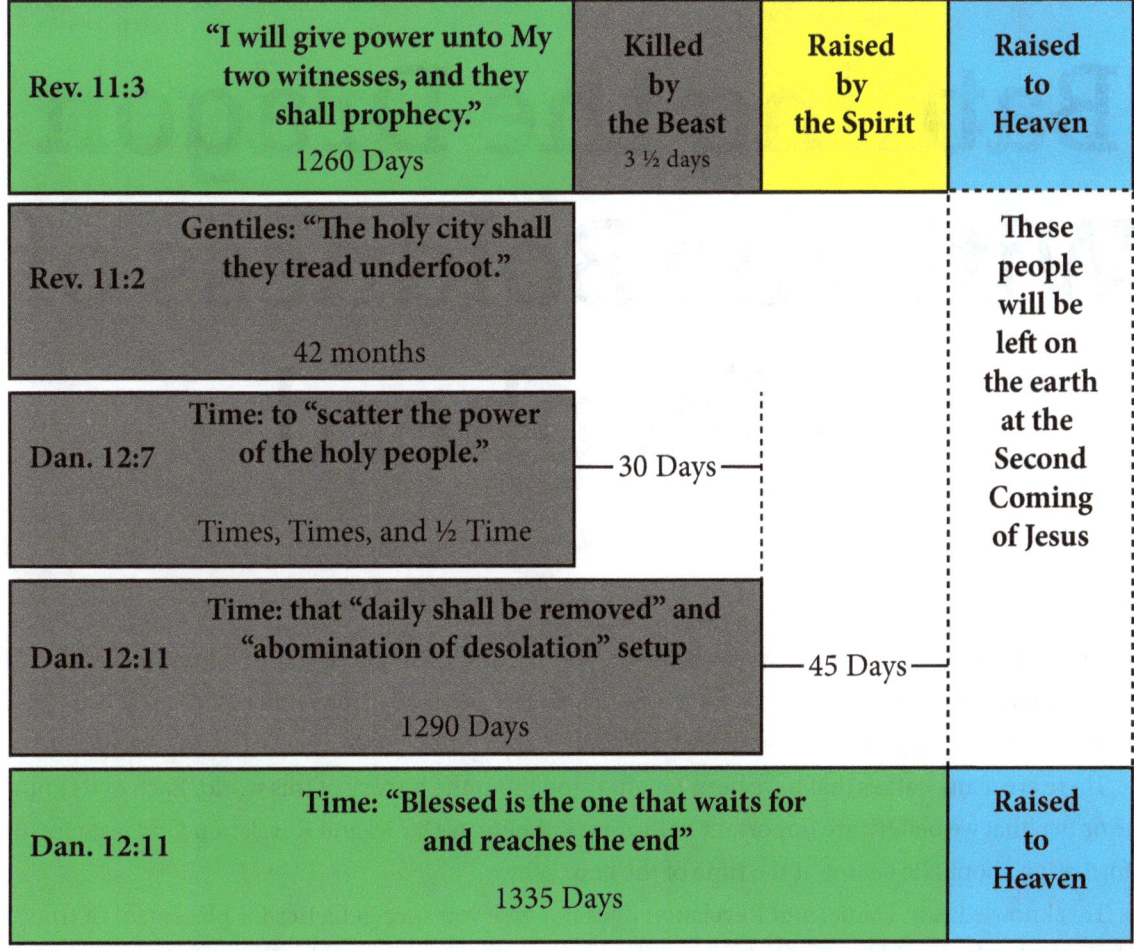

After God's witnesses, Daniel and John, are killed, Satan will remove his old system of idol worship, or paganism, and set up his new system. Gabriel tells us that Satan will stand up against Jesus and then reveals the end of the story: Satan's time will be short. Daniel 8:25 says, "he shall be broken without hand."

Daniel saw the end of sin in Nebuchadnezzar's dream: "Thou sawest till that a stone was cut out without hands, which smote the image upon his feet that were of iron and clay, and brake them to pieces. Then was the iron, the clay, the brass, the silver, and the gold, broken to pieces together, and became like the chaff of the summer threshingfloors; and the wind carried them away, that no place was found for them …" (Dan. 2:34, 35). "And in the days of these kings shall the God of heaven set up a kingdom, which shall never be destroyed: and the kingdom shall not be left to other people, but it shall break in pieces and consume all these kingdoms, and it shall stand for ever" (Dan. 2:44).

Satan's power will be broken without hand. No human being is able to stop Satan, but God can and will.

Chapter 11

Battling the Dragon With the Boldness of a Shepherd

"If you know the enemy and know yourself, you need not fear the result of a hundred battles. If you know yourself but not the enemy, for every victory gained you will also suffer a defeat. If you know neither the enemy nor yourself, you will succumb in every battle," wrote Sun Tzu in *The Art of War*.

There are many battles that have been fought throughout the history of this world. Each of us know one or two that we believe are important in history. But here in Daniel and Revelation God is giving us information about His enemy at the time of the end. Why?

This knowledge in Daniel and Revelation does not give you special tactics for placement of troops or how the battle should be directed. They tell you about the character and actions of His enemy. God is giving you information that is vital to the salvation of each man and woman. It is knowledge that you need for the crisis of all ages at the time of the end. Let's illustrate this principle with a famous story.

King Saul declared war with the Philistines because they had invaded the land of Judah and were destroying and pilfering at will. He gathered his troops together and met the enemy at the Valley of Elah. This valley was located in a key location on the road between the sea coast and the city of Jerusalem. Here the Philistines were blocked from advancing to the city of Jerusalem by the army of Israel.

Instead of immediately advancing and fighting, the leader of the Philistines toys with Israel as a cat toys with a mouse. He sends his best warrior to deliver a message to the men of Israel. Send one soldier and he and I will fight to the death. The side of the loser will become slaves to the winner. Is this not the way of each contest that you have witnessed? Each competitor says: *I am better than you and I can prove it. I am faster, stronger and smarter than you.* That premise is the basis for the Olympics and other sports. But this story is not about who will win the gold metal. The Philistines wanted their vanquished foe to be their slaves. To their slaves, they will dictate their work, their tribute, and their religion. Freedom of speech, work, and religion will be stripped from them.

The Bible account tells us that the Israelites looked at the strength and stature of the warrior and trembled. Forty days later these two armies were given a lesson that they would not forget. They were witnesses of how God overcomes in the battle against evil.

What was Goliath's challenge? "I defy the armies of Israel this day; give me a man, that we may fight together. When Saul and all Israel heard those words of the Philistine, they were dismayed, and greatly afraid" (1 Sam. 17:10, 11).

His challenge was simple. We are stronger than you are, and our god is stronger than yours. How did the armies of Israel react? "And all the men of Israel, when they saw the man, fled from him, and were sore afraid" (1 Sam. 17:24). They considered his strength, and then they considered their own. He was taller and stronger and had better weapons. They looked at each other and waited for someone to volunteer, but no one stepped forward. They told each other to pray about it and decide the next day. In other words, they are hiding in plain sight.

Then a young shepherd arrived in camp. He saw and heard the giant. He asked, "What is going on? Which of you men of Israel is planning to fight this giant?" The soldiers asked David: "Have ye seen this man that is come up? surely to defy Israel is he come up: and it shall be, that the man who killeth him, the king will enrich him with great riches, and will give him his daughter, and make his father's house free in Israel" (1 Sam. 17:25).

David asked them one thing more: "…who is this uncircumcised Philistine, that he should defy the armies of the living God?" (1 Sam. 17:26). David's question changes our thinking about the situation. Do the men of Israel not understand that this giant is challenging the God of Israel? Do they not realize that they represent God?

Do any of these seasoned soldiers volunteer at this point in the narrative? No. Do you understand that this youth has just schooled the men of the army of Israel?

David's elder brother hears his little brother's questions. How could David question the courage of the army of Israel? He says to himself, "I'll take care of this youngster!" David's next question hits his elder brother right between the eyes: "What have I now done? Is there not a cause?" (1 Sam. 17:29).

David's question is simple. "Is there not a cause?" He was saying, "Should we not battle against this giant? Should we not make a stand against paganism? Should we not defend the honor of the God of Israel?" Do you suppose that David's elder brother understood? Did his brother learn the lesson that day? Did he make a decision to meet the giant? David's brother made a decision, but it was not to fight the giant.

What does David do after he talks with his brother? "He walked over to some others and asked them the same thing and received the same answer" (1 Sam. 17:30, NLT). What did David do? What did David ask these soldiers of God? Who will go? Who will fight this giant? He is looking for the faithful one who will fight for God's cause. But something is happening in the camp of Saul. "And when the words were heard which David spake, they rehearsed them before Saul: and he sent for him" (1 Sam. 17:31).

Standing before the king, David asks, "Who will fight this giant that defies the living God?" Saul responds as did the others. "The giant is huge, but the man who kills him will be given riches." David realizes that there is no one—not even the king—who is willing to fight the giant. It is at that point that David makes his decision. "And David said to Saul, Let no man's heart fail because of him; thy servant will go and fight with this Philistine" (1 Sam. 17:32). The king questions David's action, but David tells the king why he is willing to fight the giant:

> And David said unto Saul, Thy servant kept his father's sheep, and there came a lion, and a bear, and took a lamb out of the flock: And I went out after him, and smote him, and delivered it out of his mouth: and when he arose against me, I caught him by his beard, and smote him, and slew him. Thy servant slew both the lion and the bear: and this uncircumcised Philistine shall be as one of them, seeing he hath defied the armies of the living God. (1 Sam. 17:34–36)

These experiences have led David to conclude in faith: "The LORD that delivered me out of the paw of the lion, and out of the paw of the bear, he will deliver me out of the hand of this Philistine" (1 Sam. 17:37).

David understood the cause. "The LORD He is God. The LORD He is God." He is next to me, delivering me in every situation, helping me with every problem, and standing with me to fight every giant. He is the One who will protect me and guide me when I battle this giant. He is the One who will deliver me out of the hand of this giant.

David is schooling the king of Israel. The king understands and says to David, "Go, and the LORD be with thee" (1 Sam. 17:37). Did the king volunteer to go against the giant? Did he learn his lesson? No. David leaves the king and approaches the giant.

> And the Philistine said unto David, Am I a dog, that thou comest to me with staves? And the Philistine cursed David by his gods. And the Philistine said to David, Come to me, and I will give thy flesh unto the fowls of the air, and to the beasts of the field.

Then said David to the Philistine, Thou comest to me with a sword, and with a spear, and with a shield: but I come to thee in the name of the LORD of hosts, the God of the armies of Israel, whom thou hast defied. (1 Sam. 17:43–45)

Before the battle begins, David schools the giant and us: "I am here as a representative of the God of heaven. He is the God of the armies of Israel. He is the One you have defied and to whom you will answer." He is schooling the giant and all the Philistines who are within earshot. He is schooling the king and all the men of Israel. He is schooling all who read this story.

Do David's words burn in your heart? They should. This should be the battle cry of every member of God's host. We are representatives of God and part of His army. We must be ready to stand for God when a cause arises.

Then David issues the giant, the Philistines, and the men of Israel a prophecy.

> This day will the Lord deliver thee into mine hand; and I will smite thee, and take thine head from thee; and I will give the carcases of the host of the Philistines this day unto the fowls of the air, and to the wild beasts of the earth; that all the earth may know that there is a God in Israel. And all this assembly shall know that the Lord saveth not with sword and spear: for the battle is the Lord's, and he will give you into our hands. (1 Sam. 17:45–47)

Is David careful with his words? No, he unapologetically tells the giant that he will die for the words he has spoken against the God of Israel and his army will be slaughtered because of their actions against the God of Israel. "All the earth will know," he says, "that there is a God in Israel, because you will be defeated today. All the earth will know that the Lord He is God. We are His people and the sheep of His pasture."

You know the rest of the story. David advanced and conquered the giant. The army of Israel advanced and conquered. It was a great victory for the God of Israel.

But this story would not have happened were it not for David's faith. He had seen God lead in his life. God had taught David in the hills of Bethlehem. He had nourished his faith and sent him to the armies of Israel at just the right time. He led him to ask the right questions of the king and led him to the field of battle against the giant. God gave David the victory.

What is our lesson in all this? David believed the God who led him in the past would be by his side in the battle with the giant and help him overcome the enemy of God. In other words, what God did with David He can do with you.

The time is coming when we will have to stand like David. We will have to recognize the cause of God. We will have to ask the right questions and lead the people of God down the right path. John points to this time when he describes the serpent casting water out of his mouth as a flood after the woman that he might cause her to be carried away of a flood (Rev. 12:15). The serpent is the enemy of God. He will try to drown the church of God with words, doctrines, and miracles, but God has an answer: "When the enemy shall come in like a flood, the Spirit of the Lord shall lift up a standard against him" (Isa. 59:19). When the enemy of God stands before the church of God and demands a battle to the death, we will recognize the cause. We will recognize him as the enemy of God and will teach the enemy a thing or two. We will identify ourselves as children of God. We will then remind the enemy that Jesus "will crush your head" (Gen. 3:15, NIV).

How will you respond? God has given us the prophecies of Daniel and Revelation. These prophecies are to be carried to the four corners of the earth by the riders on the four horses (Rev. 6). The prophecies unmask God's enemies and their activities during the time of the end (Rev. 12, 13, and 17). It is time to put on God's armor:

> Put on the whole armour of God, that ye may be able to stand against the wiles of the devil. For we wrestle not against flesh and blood, but against principalities, against powers, against the rulers of the darkness of this world, against spiritual wickedness in high places. (Eph. 6:11, 12)

Then we are told to advance to victory:

> The Christian's warfare is not a warfare waged against flesh and blood, but against principalities, against powers, against spiritual wickedness in high places. The Christian must contend with supernatural forces, but he is not to be left alone to engage in the conflict. The Saviour is the captain of his salvation, and with Him man may be more than conqueror.
>
> The world's Redeemer would not have man in ignorance of Satan's devices. The vast confederacy of evil is arrayed against those who would overcome; but Christ would have us look to the things that are not seen, to the armies of heaven that encamp round about those who love God, to deliver them. The angels of heaven are interested in behalf of men. The power of Omnipotence is at the service of those who trust in God. The Father accepts the righteousness of Christ in behalf of his followers, and they are surrounded with light and holiness which Satan cannot penetrate. The voice of the Captain of our salvation speaks to his followers, saying, "'Be of good cheer; I have overcome the world.' I am your defense; advance to victory." (Ellen G. White, *Review and Herald*, July 1, 1890)

This is our cause. We are to advance to victory, for this is the will of God.

We invite you to view the complete
selection of titles we publish at:

www.AspectBooks.com

Scan with your mobile
device to go directly
to our website.

Please write or email us your praises, reactions, or
thoughts about this or any other book we publish at:

P.O. Box 954
Ringgold, GA 30736

info@AspectBooks.com

Aspect Books titles may be purchased in bulk for
educational, business, fund-raising, or sales promotional use.
For information, please e-mail

BulkSales@AspectBooks.com

Finally, if you are interested in seeing
your own book in print, please contact us at

publishing@AspectBooks.com

We would be happy to review your manuscript for free.

www.ingramcontent.com/pod-product-compliance
Lightning Source LLC
Chambersburg PA
CBHW080251170426
43192CB00014BA/2634